D1050357

"Having known Edmund Chan for a number of privileged to see his ministry and that of the ch quarters, I know of his calibre and the quality of his mentoring ministry. And I can wholeheartedly endorse it and welcome the distillation of his years of experience contained in this book."

Dr. Stuart Briscoe
Minister at Large
Elmbrook Church
"Telling the Truth" Ministries

"Nobody is more qualified to speak on mentoring and disciplemaking than Edmund Chan. The concepts in this book, if followed, have the potential to change the paradigm for how you live and minister. Edmund is paving the way for a whole new and desperately-needed disciplemaking paradigm in today's world. The principles in this book have not only been tried and applied by the staff of Covenant Evangelical Free Church but are thoroughly biblical and needed if we are going to see true transformation in our ministries. I could not recommend this book and its content more highly and am making it available to each of my staff. I recommend that you do the same."

Dr. Timothy J. Addington
Senior Vice President, EFCA
Executive Director, ReachGlobal

"I have greatly benefited from the mentoring of Pastor Edmund Chan. The mentoring curriculum has been refreshing – his heart for God, his profound grasp of the Scriptures, his love for the Church and his perceptive observations of the world. The principles in this book are life on life in life – the essence of mentoring at its best – and I heartily recommend it to you."

Dr. Geoff Gorsuch
Director of Men's Ministry
The Navigators

"As I read these reflections of Edmund Chan, my heart exploded with the Spirit of God proclaiming, 'This is my truth and my wisdom.' He shares with us how to have a deep walk with God, lead with God's heart, and impact the next generation."

Kent Humphreys
Ambassador
Fellowship of Companies for Christ International

"What a gem of a book on mentoring paradigms! Edmund passionately preaches what he consistently practices. Having had the joy of being one of his early mentors, I know this to be so. And having attended – and enjoyed – some Monday QC sessions, I can affirm that his staff members are an example of a learning community with the senior pastor as a mentor par excellence.

The primary need of the church is leadership – leaders with vision, who are growing deep in God. Edmund Chan is meeting this need as a gifted visionary leader and a mentor of leaders. God has, through divine appointments, enabled Edmund to mentor leaders in various arenas of life beyond Singapore and Asia. He already has a global legacy of leaders who are intentionally mentoring others. That's the outcome of his 'thinking big, starting small and building deep'!"

Jim Chew
Asia-Pacific Missions Leader
The Navigators

"It is my distinct privilege to commend this short but profound book of my pastor, mentor, and friend to you. I see these not just as 'paradigms' for our consideration, but as 'gems' for our inspiration and transformation. Presumably, Rev. Edmund Chan wrote these 30 paradigms to be commensurate with the 30 years of Covenant Evangelical Free Church's history. But knowing this 'pastor of pastors', they only represent a fraction of the cumulative wisdom which he has gleaned through his years as a respected pastor and a sought-after mentor of the leaders in our city. These weighty paradigms are the fruits of the deep theological reflection of someone with a firm grasp of God's Word, forged in the crucible of deep compassion and authentic love for God's people, especially for those with leadership responsibilities in God's Kingdom."

Dr. Ho Chiao Ek
Principal
East Asia School of Theology
Singapore

"This interesting and highly readable book by Edmund Chan provides a spiritual blueprint. It offers a compass for effective Christian living and service. Using neat alliterations, pithy statements, and clear ideas – all aimed at helping the reader understand and remember key principles – the book invites readers to apply and flesh out the blueprint in their daily lives and in their Christian communities. The principles and ideas offered in the book have emerged from the life and witness of a vibrant congregation led by an able pastor and his team. There are many gems in the book waiting to be discovered."

Bishop Robert Solomon
The Methodist Church
Singapore

"Mentoring is a buzzword of today not only for the ministry of the church but also for the marketplace. However, this has been a passion for Pastor Edmund since the beginning of his Christian ministry. He has studied the process, practiced it and taught it to many. These 30 key paradigms are precious gems distilled from lessons learnt over the years of faithful mentoring of lives. This book is a treasure trove of truths that will help every pastor as well as marketplace minister in reproducing lives for the glory of God."

Apostle Lawrence Khong
Senior Pastor
Faith Community Baptist Church
Singapore

"A comprehensive guide to Mentoring that lays out excellent principles of leadership and discipleship. Packed with tremendous insight and candour, Mentoring Paradigms brings us back to focus on the fundamentals of living out our purpose as leaders of today's generation."

Rev. Dr. Kong Hee
Founder–Senior Pastor
City Harvest Church
Singapore

"Leaders understand the importance of mentoring. However, few understand that the main and continual ministry of great leaders is one of mentoring leaders. And then there are even fewer that know how, and in what, to mentor the leaders under them. In Mentoring Paradigms, Edmund Chan, known as a leader and authority in the area of mentoring, gives to any leader with a serious desire to mentor 30 invaluable areas to focus on. This book will cause the reader to first be confronted with the question "are these things a part of my life?" before he is able to consider mentoring someone else in them."

Rev. Dr. Rick Seaward
Apostolic Overseer
Victory Family Center
Singapore

"Few authors can cover so much breadth and depth in so few words. My good friend, Edmund, belongs to that unique species and does it with élan and elegance. He has put together three crucial anchors of Christian development, that of mentoring, leadership and discipleship. When these three anchors are carefully nurtured to circumscribe our life and living, then we are ready to develop a whole generation of servants of Christ with depth; who will go the full distance with a divine sense of destiny. For this we have Pastor Edmund to thank. His years of gleanings, insights and wisdom have now been made available to a wider audience!"

Dr. Daniel Ho
Senior Pastor, Damansara Utama Methodist Church (DUMC)
Malaysia

"In Mentoring Paradigms, widely influential Singaporean pastor Edmund Chan reveals some of the secrets of success of his own amazing ministry. With an extraordinary economy of words memorably signposted to show the way, he goes deeper to take us higher. Digging into and applying the mine of truths within this book may not only transform your ministry but you as well! But isn't that the way it's supposed to be?"

Dr. Stuart Robinson
Founding Pastor, Crossway Baptist Church
Melbourne, Australia

"This is vintage Edmund Chan! The mentoring paradigms that Edmund outlines in this book are poignant and powerful. They address vital issues that are more substructure then superstructure (to borrow the terms used in the first mentoring paradigm in this book). I have personally benefitted from these paradigms, having processed some of them with Edmund in our own mentoring times together. So I know they work; not just as paradigms, but in practice. Thanks, Edmund for putting them down succinctly on paper. Now in turn, we can pass them on to those we have the privilege to mentor."

Rev. Benny Ho
Senior Pastor, Faith Community Church
Founder, Arrows School of Ministry
Perth, Australia

Mentoring PARADIGMS

REFLECTIONS ON MENTORING, LEADERSHIP AND DISCIPLESHIP

EDMUND CHAN

MENTORING PARADIGMS:
Reflections on Mentoring, Leadership and Discipleship

Copyright © Covenant Evangelical Free Church, 2008

Published by
Lifestyle Impact Ministries
Kent Humphreys
PO Box 271054
Oklahoma City, OK 73137-1054
Phone: 405-949-0070 x102 or 405-917-1681 x102
Email: kent@fcci.org or khumphreys@ahpartners.com
Website: www.lifestyleimpact.com

In Partnership with:
Covenant Evangelical Free Church
167 Jalan Bukit Merah
Tower 5 #17-10
Singapore 150167
Tel: (65) 6892 6811
Fax: (65) 6892 1502
Email: resources@cefc.org.sg
Website: www.cefc.org.sg

To the late Doug Sparks of the Navigators.
This man of God was one of my most influential early mentors.
I miss our regular 'man-to man' times when he often began with:

"So, what's your question?"

Acknowledgments

Books are often the work of a team. What would leaders do without them!

I would be sorely remiss if I did not thank my colleagues who pilgrimaged with me in our weekly QC Time and expressed their thoughts on my paradigms that they heard me impart over the years.

There are two who helped beyond the call of duty. Laura Chao, my editor, who worked late without grumbling to accommodate my own deadlines in the midst of the heavy demands of pastoral leadership. And Pastor Tan Kay Kiong, my wing-man, who sacrificed his time in London to valiantly grapple with the early manuscript.

Finally, my deep appreciation to Ann Chan for writing the foreword. That alone would have had my sincere gratitude. But that she went beyond that and took the opportunity to express her esteem and love for me is a grace most undeserved, and thus most cherished. Thank you, my love.

CONTENTS

On Discipleship

Foreword

Authors usually invite an esteemed figure, or an authority in the field, to write the foreword for their book. Which author would ever think of asking their own spouse to write a foreword?

Edmund Chan would!

And it was not something he did on the spur of the moment either. He had told me years ago that if he should ever publish his thoughts, he would want me to write a foreword for at least one of his books. I laughed. But he was serious of course. And I shouldn't have been that surprised when he asked me this time.

You see, Edmund Chan is an intellectual radical.

He quietly reasoned with me that apart from God, no one knows him better than his wife. I can't argue with that! And to charm me into it, he said that I was his faithful co-labourer in ministry and his esteemed best friend.

How could I possibly win an argument with him when he put it across with such powers of persuasion? So I agreed.

Mentoring is Edmund's passion. The Lord has graciously blessed him with a vast number of people he has personally impacted and influenced through mentoring, some of whom would read like a Who's Who list in the Kingdom. But the remarkable thing is that he has never sought them out. God brought each one to him by divine appointment!

And he would skillfully and discerningly point each one along their way with wisdom that is quite beyond his years. It is not surprising then that many of his mentorees are older than he is. Yet they recognize and resonate with the solid principles he masterfully articulates.

So where does he glean his wisdom from? No doubt, it is a gift from God. In Edmund's own words, a "sacred trust". Nonetheless, on the human side of the equation, he is an avid reader, a reflective thinker and a life-long learner. Over the years, he has diligently made time for personal reflection. His personal Think-Time as he calls it.

This book is a product of his keen reflection. Each idea or paradigm can be further unpacked and explored; affirmed or argued over; torn apart and put together again. It is not meant to be the final word on the topic. Knowing my husband, it would probably take a book for each of his paradigms! But he has chosen to state them as briefly as possible, simply to stimulate thinking.

Thus, may you have a joyous journey of not just reading but thinking through and applying these paradigms in your life.

I have been an unabashed fan of his insightful teachings. I have often encouraged him to put his thoughts in print. But he is, by his own admission, "one of the world's most reluctant authors". He loves books. He loves to think through them. And he esteems great authors so much that he wants others to read them, not him. Recently, on his 50th birthday, his staff asked him to name 50 books he has read. He did it with relish!

But for what it's worth, I'm glad he wrote this book. What I wasn't too keen on was writing a foreword to it! Now that I have finished my humble foreword, I hope you don't find me too forward in my esteem of the author. He is after all my beloved husband and my wise mentor!

With gratitude,
Ann Chan
Associate Pastor
Covenant Evangelical Free Church

Introduction

QC Time. This is one of the chief highlights of my week as a senior pastor.

Some years ago, I asked my pastoral staff: "Why do pastors take a day off on Monday?" They smiled. Knowing that I believe in the principle of Sabbath-keeping, they wondered what I had in mind. "Monday is not a good day for pastors to rest," I said with mock seriousness. There is some truth in it nonetheless.

I went on to explain two things.

First, because of adrenalin overflow after an intense weekend of ministry, many pastors 'rest' on Monday in a restless sort of way. Their adrenalin is still high and their engines are still in overdrive. Let's tap into that!

Second, tapping into that creative energy is not about doing more work. I wanted to cultivate a learning culture. It's about reflecting more. I sought to establish a learning community of reflective practitioners!

Hence, I started QC Time on Monday mornings.

QC stands for two things. It asks, "So what's your **question?**" and "What's your **contribution?**" The pastoral and ministry staff are encouraged to ask any question that they might have on life and ministry. Everyone contributes by either refining the question or offering their perspective on it. And they often do so with such spontaneous humour that there is much laughter at our QC Time!

One of the significant benefits of our QC Time is a solid pulpit ministry.

I start each Monday morning with the question, *"So how was the sermon yesterday?"* We evaluate the sermon while it is still fresh in our minds. Then I have the preaching staff for the next Sunday share his or her sermon outline. And the rest of us contribute to it. Thus, staff members complete their sermon outline by early *Monday* morning. There is no *Saturday Night Fever* in our sermon preparation!

Another significant benefit of our QC Time is mentoring.

As a mentoring senior pastor, I leverage the prevailing questions at QC Time to impart key lessons for life and ministry. I share candidly from my pilgrimage and reflection. Over the years, I have faithfully shared with the staff these **mentoring paradigms** gleaned from my personal think-time. It has been beneficial in mentoring a learning organization.

To celebrate our *30th* church anniversary, I would like to succinctly present *30* vital mentoring lessons from our QC Time together over the years. This little book deals primarily with reflections on mentoring, leadership and discipleship. It is a humble offering of personal ministry reflections.

My simple aim is to provoke more reflection. I want to encourage the mentoring of more reflective practitioners and the nurturing of learning organisations in Christian ministry.

So, what's *your* **Q**uestion?
And what's *your* **C**ontribution?

Have a blessed pilgrimage ahead!

In Him,
Rev Edmund Chan
Senior Pastor
Covenant Evangelical Free Church

Mentoring

TRANSFORMATION

NW

SW

NE

SE

PARADIGM 1
Mentoring the Foundation of Life:
Superstructure, Structures and Substructure

We tend to ignore what cannot be seen.

Immortalized in movies from *Sleepless in Seattle* to *King Kong*, the Empire State Building is one of the world's most recognizable skyscrapers. But while tourists snap furiously at its superstructure – the distinctive tower and Art Deco architecture – the most important element, the substructure which enables the edifice to rise to its magnificent height, is entirely ignored – because it is completely unseen.

In life, we gravitate toward the visible and the spectacular.

We judge and pride ourselves upon our influence and accomplishments. Though gratifying, this outward superstructure is however not where our primary energies should be expended.

It is in the **substructure**, the unseen foundation, that our true strength lies.

Without a deep and secure substructure, the structures cannot hold. And the superstructures cannot rise to great heights without peril. That is why more time is always spent on the foundation than on the superstructure. The wise mentor does not neglect mentoring the substructure of life. Who we are, what we do when no one sees, form the substructure of our life.

A life of worship, lived before God in the fear of Him and held together by humility, wisdom and perseverance, constitutes a foundation that will withstand immense stress and strain. The continued maintenance and growth of this substructure, firmly anchored in God through the practice of the spiritual disciplines, is the work of a lifetime.

Built upon the substructure are the **structures** – the supporting beams and columns – which fit together to form the framework around which the facade and usable floor area are built. These structures are the areas that we need to guard in our personal life. Time with family. Time with kindred-spirit friends. Time in the community of God's people. Without these in their proper places, the building would be a haphazard jumble of awkward planes and dead space.

The **superstructure** represents the outward accomplishments of our life and ministry. It is built by competence and skill. It is established by working excellently, as unto the Lord, in obedience and faithfulness. It is worthy only when the substructure is solid and the surface structures are set in place – for it is upon these that the strength, beauty and permanence of the superstructure depend.

Indeed, when we take care of the depth of our lives, God will take care of the breadth of our work and ministry.

Questions for Reflection

1. Read 1 Samuel 13:1-14. What substructures and structures were lacking in Saul's life? What effect did this have on the superstructure of his life?

2. What have you been spending the most time and conscious effort in building – the substructure, the structures or the superstructure of your life? Why?

3. What do you think God is leading you to focus on building at this point in time? How can you build in this area?

Personal
REFLECTIONS

Mentoring the Orientation of Life:
Red Bar, Blue Bar

We live in a world that applauds those in the limelight.

The world's limelight shines on successful people. Its yardstick for success is often focused on our **affluence** or **acquisitions** (what we have), our **associations** (who we know), our **appearance** (how we look), our **abilities** (what we can do) and our **accomplishments** (what we have done). These are the external, temporal measures.

Life can therefore be oriented in one of two ways.

We can orientate life around the external or the internal. Our life's orientation can be reflected, like a bar chart, with two color-coded bars – a red bar and a blue bar. The red bar represents the external. And the blue bar the internal.

The red bar is the default way of the world. Like a flashy red Ferrari, the red-bar person measures life by the world's yardstick. Success is superficially determined by the person's accomplishments or net worth. The red bar gravitates towards the outward.

We need a radical re-definition of success in life.

The blue bar is the discipleship way of God. Like the deep blue sea, the blue-bar person celebrates deeper things. Things like integrity, character and the posture of the surrendered soul. It is a life that seeks to grow from the inside out. It gravitates towards the inward.

In life, we need both the red and blue bars; both the accomplished superstructures of life as well as the solid substructure of life. We need both the stature and the substance of the person to reflect their true status in life.

What follows on the next page are fifteen comparative indicators of red-bar and blue-bar people:

A Red-Bar Person	A Blue-Bar Person
Focuses on **Externals**	Focuses on the **Inner Life**
Values **Accomplishments**	Values **Authenticity**
Values **Performance and Results**	Values **Growth and Learning**
Puts **Competence** first	Puts **Character** first
Does Good with the aim of **Looking Good**	Does Good as an outflow of **Being Good**
Esteems **Status and Stature**	Esteems **Substance**
Is **Competitive and Boastful**	Genuinely **Celebrates others**
Craves **Attention/Approval**	Is **Self-effacing**
Insecure without the limelight	Has a **Quiet Confidence/** Security
Is **Stressed and Flustered**	Is **Steady and Calm**
Reacts to criticism	**Responds** to criticism
Cannot let go of **Control**	**Empowers** others
Is **Restless** in spirit	Is **Rested** in spirit
Display: Outward Show	**Depth:** Inward Security
Default way of the world	**Discipleship way** of God

When the red bar supersedes the blue bar (when **competence** and **accomplishment** are emphasised above **character** and **authenticity**) we subtly compromise the development of depth in life. As such, we need to develop the blue bar of life and not neglect it. Inner growth!

We live in a world that applauds red-bar accomplishments. But the wise mentor does not neglect the more important orientation of growing as a blue-bar person in a red-bar world!

Questions for Reflection

1. Which mark(s) of the red bar has been a struggle for you? Which mark(s) of the blue bar would you consider an area of growth?

2. Why does Jesus call us to a blue-bar life?

3. How can we prevent ourselves from making the blue bar a red-bar achievement (i.e. taking pride in our inner life and comparing it with others')?

Personal REFLECTIONS

Mentoring the Foundation of Leadership:
Status, Stature and Substance

It is the substance of a leader that ultimately defines the leader.

Sometimes we hear the lament: "He has the *status* of leadership but not the *stature* of a leader." Even so, it is the *substance* of a leader that ultimately defines the leader.

Our **status** in leadership refers to the titles that we have and the positions that we hold. The **stature** of leadership comprises two aspects: our credibility (how others view us) and our confidence (how we view ourselves). But of far greater importance is our **substance** (how God views us).

The iceberg is an apt analogy. What is seen above the water represents our status and stature. What lies beneath represents our substance, forming the greater part of who we are (what is seen by God).

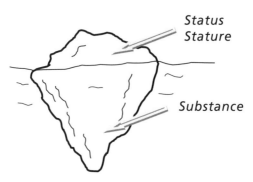

Status
Stature

Substance

In our performance-driven society, people are only interested in our status – the titles and positions that they think represent us. As a result, we focus our efforts on striving for higher status. We often miss out on developing the stature which builds confidence and credibility. Surely, status without stature is hollow.

But it is the **substance** within us that matters most to God.

When we are people of substance, we live beyond mere status and stature. We cultivate an emotional stability and restedness, security and humility, which enable us to handle crises, criticisms and compliments well.

At the heart of our status, stature and substance lies our sense of security. But *true inner security*, where we can be small yet secure, is the true expression of substance in leadership.

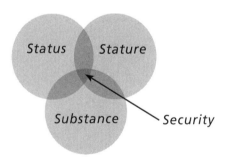

Ultimately, God is more interested in what we have become rather than merely what we have accomplished for Him.

When we develop and grow in substance, the status and stature of leadership will be built on solid ground. We will then live with **A**uthenticity in our worship, **B**rokenness in our walk and **C**ourage in our work.

A wise mentor understands what ultimately defines us as leaders. Substance!

Questions for Reflection

1. Was Paul's leadership based on status, stature or substance? How so? (Phil 3:4-14)?

2. Why would our substance help us handle crises, criticisms and compliments better than our status and stature?

3. In a society where upward mobility is perceived to be the measure of our success, how can we live as people of substance who are small yet secure?

Personal
REFLECTIONS

Mentoring the Inner Life:
Nothing to Prove, Nothing to Lose and Nothing to Hide

Nothing to prove is a state of deep security in God.
Nothing to lose is a state of absolute surrender to God.
Nothing to hide is a state of true integrity before God.

The root cause of our inability to reach this blessed state is our lack of inner security. Insecurity causes us to fall into a performance trap. Performance-drivenness leads to fragile egos. It causes us to make vain comparisons. Envy and jealousy subtly rear their ugly heads.

Envy and jealousy are not the same. Envy is desiring what others have because we don't have it. Jealousy happens when others have what we have – but more!

As a result, we often find it difficult to celebrate others' strengths and successes. Cain measured his offering against Abel's and couldn't understand why God rejected his offering since both were "first fruits" offerings. In his insecure jealousy, he murdered Abel. Pride got in the way.

The key to living with **nothing to prove** is humility.

Philippians 2:3 says, *"Do nothing out of selfish ambition or vain conceit, but in humility consider others better than yourselves."* If there were something we wanted to prove, it should be that God's surpassing strength is made perfect in our weakness.

In life, Humility and Surrender walk hand in hand in a common pilgrimage.

Yet we struggle to give up our rights and desires. Insecurity leads to a fear of full surrender. Instead, we seek in vain to find our security in acquiring, possessing and hoarding. In maintaining control. Losing all for the sake of Christ begins to terrify us. We don't mind making sacrifices but we are afraid of fully surrendering ourselves to God. We forget that surrender is not about **giving up**; it's about **giving in** to God.

In truth, we have become possessed by our possessions. Controlled by our need for control. We miss the point that true security comes when we find satisfaction only in Christ. When we come to this realization, we can surrender all and live with **nothing to lose**.

When Christ is absolutely **everything**, then Christ alone is absolutely **enough**.

Finally, insecurity also causes us to camouflage our sins with artificial, guilt-soothing human constructs. We hide our heartaches, sins and pains behind smiling masks and ministry activities. We focus on temporarily managing our sins instead of completely repenting of them – and thus finding our freedom in the mighty transformation in Jesus.

When we walk in true repentance, then there is **nothing to hide**.

D.L. Moody once said, "Moses spent forty years thinking he was somebody. He spent the next forty years learning he was nobody. He spent the last forty years discovering what God can do with a nobody."

Indeed, God can do wonderful things with a nobody. A nobody with nothing to prove, nothing to lose and nothing to hide!

Questions for Reflection

1. Read 1 Samuel 10-12. What was King Saul trying to "prove" and "hide" in these three chapters?

2. Read Philippians 3:7-10. What was Paul's one aspiration?

3. What does having "nothing to prove, nothing to lose, nothing to hide" mean to you in your present circumstances?

Personal
REFLECTIONS

Mentoring a Sense of Destiny:
Three Grand Pursuits In Life

The problem is that we often micro-manage our lives.

People seek direction in life. What we desperately need however is a profound sense of destiny. We can't or won't see the big picture. We are inclined to think short-term rather than go for the long haul.

We desperately seek our direction but almost completely ignore our destiny.

A sense of destiny does at least two things for us. It orientates us towards the big picture of life. And it steers us towards the long haul. Going for the long haul rather than the short-term is a defining mark of wisdom.

What then does living with a sense of destiny involve? It calls us to a grand adventure. It is a calling to three primary pursuits in life:

The God We Are to Know

God invites us to know Him. It has often been said that ***knowing God*** and ***knowing about God*** are two different things. God has revealed Himself for this very purpose: that we might know about Him. And grow to know Him personally and intimately (John 17:3; Phil 3:10)!

The knowledge of God is compelling.

Through the redemptive love of our Lord Jesus Christ, God invites us to have an intimate relationship with Him. It is this intimate relationship that promises a life-changing experience. A growing intimacy with God draws us unto a life of obedience and freedom in Christ.

The Life We Are to Live

Life is too short to live with compromises. We all have only one life to live. Without exception. None of us can increase the length of our days. Seen from the perspective of history, life is short. A sense of destiny begins with a deep realisation of the brevity of life. It is a worthy gem of wisdom.

It was E. Stanley Jones who said, "My life in my hand is a pain and a problem; my life in God's hand is a power and a possibility!" God calls us to a glorious redemptive life with purpose and potential!

The Purpose We Are to Embrace

There is a reason why we exist. Life is too short to live aimlessly. Drifting through life on auto-cruise mode is not God's agenda for our life. We must live with the end in mind. What then is the end?

In the Church today, we tend to see the Great Commission as a mission and this mission as an end in itself. But God's true end for us is a transformed life in Christ!

That's the purpose we have to embrace! To be conformed to the image of God's Son. And the Great Commission is the *means* to redeem a lost world to accomplish that end.

That's living with a sense of destiny! We are to be a people who seek to know God.

And to make Him known!

Questions for Reflection

1. What do you wake up for each morning? What keeps you awake at night?

2. How can we know God more intimately?

3. What is your mission and calling in life?

Personal
REFLECTIONS

Mentoring With The End In Mind:
Perspective, Posture, Pragmatics and Power

Begin with the end in mind.

In Christian mentoring, we mentor with a purpose. The best mentors do not focus on the program but on the purpose. That's mentoring with the end in mind. There are four mentoring objectives towards that end.

We mentor for wisdom in thinking (perspective), brokenness in attitude (posture), competence in both life-skills and ministry-skills (pragmatics) and the experience of God's daily presence in our lives (power).

A Certain Kind of Perspective

Our worldview must undergo a radical re-orientation. We need to encounter the truth, experience the truth and embrace the truth. This happens when we immerse our minds in Scripture and tutor our hearts to obey it.

We are thus being mentored by the Scriptures.

There is no short cut to this **renewing of the mind**. It is a daily investment. Our perspectives are increasingly informed by the

Scriptures. We seek to have a perspective shaped exclusively by Scripture and by a faithful obedience to it.

A Certain Kind of Posture

It is curious to note that our Lord was never impressed with the knowledge of the Scribes and the Pharisees. He was looking out for something else beyond the *knowing*. He was looking for the *heart* (Matt 13:1–23).

There is a certain receptivity and meekness that marks true disciples (Isa 66:2). But meekness is not weakness. This is the paradox. There is a profound **humble-boldness** in a life with the right focus on God.

A certain kind of posture is thus about a brokenness of heart before God, a meekness of heart in God and an openness of heart to God.

A Certain Kind of Pragmatics

Pragmatics is intentional skill development – a disciplined and growing competence in both life-skills and ministry-skills. Disciples have a growing competency.

Life is too short to be lived without **thoughtful, skilled competence**.

When tutored individuals encounter difficult situations, they have the emotional reservoir and capacity to deal wisely with them – not react to them. And coaching these skills, not just in ministry but also in life, is what holistic mentoring is about.

A Certain Kind of Power

Power belongs to the Lord. It is a divine attribute. But in man, it is not. Power in man is a by-product; in God, it is a given. Unfortunately, it is in the disposition of fallen humanity to either grab power through pride or to shun God's power through unbelief; or both!

Because **spiritual power** is intoxicating, God's hedge for this is love.

When we are more enamoured of power than of love, we have lost our focus. True spiritual power is released from on high to build His Kingdom. In fact, God's very presence is His very power! We thus seek to abide in His daily presence. And be mentored to receive and release power judiciously in love.

Questions for Reflection

1. Do you have something to help you to grow regularly in the Scriptures?

2. Do you have the posture of humble-boldness in your life? In what way?

3. What life-skills and ministry skills would you need most in the next lap of your life?

Personal REFLECTIONS

Mentoring Core Values:
Grace, Growth and Godliness

A sound set of core values is of paramount importance.

Clearly crafted, articulated and implemented core values are an asset to individuals and organizations alike. They distinctively set us apart from others. For an organization, core values reveal the ethos and heartbeat of that organization. For an individual, his or her distinctiveness.

Of course, different people and organizations have different core values.

At our QC Time, grace, growth and godliness have constantly been affirmed to us as core values for the staff. I seek to mentor the staff in these staff core values. What then are grace, growth and godliness?

Grace As A Core Value

Grace reveals the very heart and nature of God. He looks upon us favorably and extends His unending love to undeserving people. God's greatest act of grace is to send Jesus to die for us on the cross. As a result, we are the greatest recipients of His grace.

God wants us to be **grace-receivers** and **grace-releasers**.

As grace-receivers, we relish the joy of God's grace towards us. As grace-releasers, we offer to others 'undeserved favors' in love. Otherwise, we become ungrateful recipients of God's grace towards us. Mentoring the spirit of grace helps people to grow in Christlikeness.

Growth As A Core Value

True grace is by no means indulgent. While grace is extended to another as in the giving of the benefit of doubt, true grace calls for **accountability to grow**. It is a process in which we reflect on our experiences and mistakes so that we are not blind-sided.

Growth is a necessary feature of life.

All living things grow. Growth comes when permission is given to others to speak the truth into our life. Growth is the development and the maturing of our character. It takes great diligence to grow in our faith and character. This will render us neither useless nor unfruitful in the true knowledge of God (2 Pet 1:4, 8).

Godliness As A Core Value

Lastly, when we walk in grace, we will grow in godliness. The key marker of true Christian growth is godliness. In essence, godliness is **putting God in the equation of life** – having a God-ward orientation in every sphere of life. It is a progressive work of sanctification through the Holy Spirit. Godliness does not come automatically. It takes hard work and training.

We don't merely *try* to be godly; we *train* to be godly (1 Tim 4:7). We rid ourselves of the works of the flesh and clothe ourselves with the fruit of the Spirit. We are no longer slaves to sin but slaves to righteousness. Our greatest satisfaction in our pilgrimage is for someone to say to us, "I can see in you the glory of my King."

Different people have different values. Wise mentors impart worthy values that have been a steady compass in their lives.

Questions for Reflection

1. When was the last time you received grace from God? When was the last time you extended grace to others?

2. Share a present situation (work, family or personal relationships) in which you have experienced growth in the past six months.

3. What transformation have you observed in the life of godliness (either yourself or others) that has been an encouragement to you?

Personal
REFLECTIONS

Three Arenas of Mentoring:
The Devotional, Domestic and Developmental Life

True mentoring is holistic and deep.

In mentoring, careful attention must be given to three hidden substructures in a person's life. These inner arenas often go unnoticed because they are private. Often they are hidden from public scrutiny. As such, these private arenas are easily neglected. Or else superficially examined with a cursory glance.

When this happens, serious fault-lines develop.

And if so, and we are not careful, they could be used by the devil to destroy the credibility and effectiveness of God's servants. Thus, while skill development is often given more attention in mentoring, there are deeper arenas that must nonetheless be emphasized. True mentoring is indeed holistic and deep.

We thus give due attention to the three inner arenas of the mentoree's life. The wise mentor helps to cultivate the devotional life, deepen the domestic life and empower the developmental life.

Cultivating the Devotional Life

Quiet Time does *not* automatically become easier as one grows older. In fact, it becomes harder. Why? Because one can browse through God's Word quickly and pick up a thought or two without much meditation and intimacy with God.

One can have the routine and the mere discipline without the encounter and the wonder. One can read the Word of God but miss the God of the Word. One can go on serving the Lord without devotion. Christian life and ministry can be faked all too easily. But God calls us to be authentic.

At the heart of authentic discipleship is a deep devotional life. It is at the foundation of true theology. As J.I. Packer often says, "True theology always leads to doxology!" We must mentor towards a deeper devotional life!

Deepening the Domestic Life

Appearances can be deceiving. Behind the scene of a leader's life is the family. One can deceptively lead a double life – an angel in church but a monster at home! A person cannot grow holistically because of such inconsistencies. Once this happens, hypocrisy sets in. And the double life takes over.

Another possible problem scenario is having an unsupportive spouse who prevents one from serving and fulfilling God's destiny in one's life. Often deep roots of woundedness must be surfaced and dealt with. It's sad that such a couple would find great difficulty serving as one. Mentoring the domestic life of the family is vital.

Empowering the Developmental Life

People tend to settle in their comfort zones. Often people fail to overcome areas of weakness due to fear of vulnerability or failure. This applies to many key arenas of life. It could apply to the need for physical exercise. Or personal growth through reading. Or growth in different ministry competencies and skills.

As long as the leader settles for the status quo, stagnation and lack of personal effectiveness sets in. We must not neglect to chart the necessary developmental growth areas to work on. We must aim to help our mentorees come out of their comfort zones. The best growth zones are always out of our comfort zone!

Let's get out of our comfort zones. Let's grow in depth in all arenas of our lives. And mentor likewise. With a mentoring that is deep and holistic!

Questions for Reflection

1. What causes one to live a double life? Why is consistency so difficult?

2. What is one common area of neglect in your life now?

3. What can do you do today to get out of your comfort zone and grow?

Personal
REFLECTIONS

Four Steps in Mentoring:
Discover the Truth, Apply It,
Reap the Benefits and Pass It On

Mentoring is not just an impartation of knowledge. It's about living a life!

Mentoring is an impartation of life and convictions. It is about living a life and sharing the journey. It also involves imparting values and vision, creating a new empowering belief system. All this takes time. It involves a complex process of growth. And growth takes time. And skill.

As such, many feel unqualified to mentor others. Nonetheless, there are four simple steps to help us start the journey. Don't just take step one (Discover the Truth) and immediately jump to step four (Pass It On). That's merely an impartation of knowledge.

Don't truncate the process.

The secret of life and value impartation lies in step two (Apply the Truth) and step three (Reap the Benefits). Only then can we share from the depth and authenticity of our lives. So here are the four fundamental steps to effective mentoring:

Discover the Truth

Discovery is the inspiration of living. Learning to discover is the perspiration. The first step in mentoring is to *learn* something good. Something worthwhile to pass on. Something that has been life-changing for you. To pass on the truth, we must first know the truth.

Truth serves as an anchor in our lives.

Without truth, we are adrift in a world of confusion and compromise. Ravi Zacharias insightfully commented that we live in an unseen world where truth is the most precious commodity. This ultimate truth is found in the Word of God (John 17:17).

Apply the Truth

Get this: Truth doesn't change lives. Rather, it is *truth applied* that changes lives! Jesus said that whoever hears His Words and *does them* is like the wise man who builds his house upon the rock (Matt 7:24, emphasis mine).

Truth can be insightful and even inspiring. But without action and obedience, it has no power. We must not truncate the application and jump straight to passing it on. Otherwise we reproduce after our kind: a superficial generation of those who eloquently pass on what they have not effectively applied.

Reap the Benefits

The benefits of truth applied must first be experienced so as to impart truth with authenticity. When that happens, we can teach what we practice and not run the danger of teaching others what we are not practicing ourselves.

Howard Hendricks, Professor at Dallas Theological Seminary said: "What I hear, I forget. What I see, I remember. What I do, I understand. When I understand, I change." Truly, what I *apply* brings about **understanding** and **transformation**.

Pass It On

Ultimately, our legacy in mentoring is to see a *multiplication* of lives. In the Old Testament, God's wondrous working was orally transmitted from one generation to the next. There was multiplication from one generation to another.

If we keep discovering the truth, applying the truth, and reaping the benefit, then we can pass on a legacy of truth from one generation to the next.

FOUR steps, not TWO!

Questions for Reflection

1. Why is "FOUR steps, not TWO!" important?

2. Of the FOUR steps, which speaks to your life the most? Why?

3. What are some life-changing truths that you have discovered?

Personal
REFLECTIONS

Three Core Competencies of a Mentor:
Shepherd, Teacher and Leader

Mentors, like pastors, have three critical roles.

Shepherding, teaching and leading are the three core competencies of the pastoral calling. They also apply to the role of the mentor. Mentors must develop in each of the competencies to be effective.

Let us look at the three-fold competencies:

1. The Mentor Who Shepherds

The mentor who shepherds knows the condition of the flock. He is sensitive to their needs. Not just the felt needs but the real needs as well. Like the Apostle Paul, the shepherding mentor knows how to admonish the unruly, encourage the fainthearted, help the weak and be patient with all men (1 Th 5:14).

There are 3 aspects to this shepherding role.

The first is **caring**. This is primarily edification through words and presence. As the saying goes, people do not care how much we know until they know how much we care. The second is **counseling**. This takes some training and skill. The wise mentor goes for the root rather than the superficial branches. The third is **coaching**. This involves discerning the spiritual direction for the people and coaching them with the principles (why) and the skills (how to).

2. The Mentor Who Teaches

Different people learn in different ways. Thus, the mentor who teaches does so in a variety of ways. Some learn best through doing a project together. Others by reading and personal reflection. Still others learn best by discussion or interaction. Thus, the best teaching mentors are the ones who seek efficacious teaching for all the learning types. They look for teachable moments. This might be informal times of relaxing together. Or a teachable moment might come at a time of crisis.

Also, the best teaching mentors are not merely those who give the answers. Rather, they ask the right questions.

And not only do they ask the right questions, they also give Word-centered principles. More significantly, they are committed to help their mentorees feed themselves with the Word. Instead of giving a fish to feed for a day, they teach others to fish – to feed for a lifetime!

3. The Mentor Who Leads

Mentors who lead are a rare breed. They are not merely shepherding or teaching lives. Rather, they are intentionally leading towards a destiny. Towards transformational Kingdom engagements. They boldly lead their mentorees towards all that God has called them to. They are not just mentoree-centered, they are God-centred!

Mentors who lead inspire hope and faith.

Challenging mentorees to embrace the work of God in their lives, these mentors model the way. They lead by example. There is a clear sense of passion, purpose and pursuit in the mentors' lives. These are visionary leaders who mentor.

May their tribe increase!

Questions for Reflection

1. What do you see in Christ's life as He lived as Shepherd, Leader and Teacher?

2. As a mentor, how would you rank your competencies?

3. How can you grow in your areas of strength and weakness?

Personal
REFLECTIONS

Philosophy of a Mentoring Leadership:

Think Big, Start Small, Build Deep

It is a daring philosophy of leadership.

"Think Big, Start Small, Build Deep" is a compelling watchword that comes up often in our QC Time. For us, it is a reminder to stop comparing. And to stay true and courageous to our specific calling from God. It cultivates a mentoring leadership committed to developing leaders who build to last.

"Think Big, Start Small, Build Deep" first challenges us to pursue with visionary courage our dreams from God. Yet it calls for the inner security to not despise small things. This is an important tension to balance. We are creatures of extremes. We tend to gravitate to one and ignore the other. It is both-and and not either-or!

Finally, it highlights the need for godly wisdom, in the exercise of wise leadership, to build deep. Thus, "Think Big, Start Small, Build Deep" is decidedly provocative in its grand sweep.

The Courage To Think Big

It first calls us to boldly dream BIG dreams IN God. There is a difference between dreaming big dreams FOR God and dreaming big dreams IN God. The former can be mere presumptuousness; the latter is rooted in the holy calling and divine promises.

Our view of God determines our work for Him.

Our God is a God of the impossible. Is anything too difficult for Him? By His word, the heavens and earth were created. Our God is an awesome God. Yet we tiptoe around God's throne and ask for the mundane.

If God is too small in our eyes, our work will be minute. But if He is bigger than the universe, then is anything too difficult for Him? Let's dare to do something so big that if God is not in it, we are doomed to fail.

The Security To Start Small

On the other hand, this guiding philosophy of leadership calls us to have an inner security to start small. Some great movements of God have an inconspicuous genesis. It takes a quiet disposition rested enough in God to begin on a small scale.

God is never in a hurry.

In His eternal timeline, everything will fall in its rightful place. While we think big, we must be willing to start small. Jesus said that the Kingdom of God is like a mustard seed (Matt 13:31-32). Start with what God has already blessed us with and given to us.

The Wisdom To Build Deep

Finally, this philosophy of leadership holds the tension by calling us to keep working on the fundamentals. Depth and influence are more efficacious in the long run than mere breadth and impact. We've got to get the fundamentals right!

Ultimately, what really counts is true depth.

Whether it's starting a movement or the discipling of lives, building deep is anchored in fulfilling God's fundamental calling and mission. It's fundamentally about developing a biblical worldview and depth of character. It's the wisdom of building to last.

"Think Big, Start Small, Build Deep." A daring philosophy of leadership. Are we courageous enough, secure enough and wise enough to pursue it?

Questions for Reflection

1. What do you think of this "Think Big, Start Small, Build Deep" philosophy?

2. Why is the philosophy so important?

3. There are three parts to the philosophy. Which part speaks to you the most and what practical steps will you take to put it into practice?

Personal REFLECTIONS

Leading with Intentionality:
By Design or By Default

Wise intentionality is the practiced skill of a mentoring leader.

During QC Time, I often remind my staff to live and lead "by design, not by default". When a leader operates by design, he is doing something with purpose and intentionality. It is carrying out an action knowing clearly why you are doing it, and what, by that action, you seek to achieve.

In contrast, when a leader operates by default, he does so without much thinking and reflection. It is carrying out an action without knowing why you are doing it and what, by that action, you seek to achieve. Doing something by default is merely going through the motions.

People and Church are complex. Just because something has worked before does not mean it will work again. We must be careful of a one-size-fits-all mentality, which is often a reflection of leadership by default rather than by design. Here's a succinct checklist for intentional leadership by design.

Checklist: Leadership by Design and not by Default

- Intentional Leaders have a sound set of core values and governing principles that guide their thinking and decisions. They do not lead by impulse or moods.

- Intentional Leaders do not feel rushed or pressured to make a hasty decision. They consider principles, priorities and future implications.

- Intentional Leaders consult with key stakeholders. They do not merely depend on their own assessments of past precedence or practices.

- Intentional Leaders are intentional and purposeful in their words and actions to help people grow. They do not try to play God by engineering circumstances to test or to hurt intentionally.

- Intentional Leaders nurture and mentor their team members towards inner-life growth and depth. They do not use them to achieve their ends.

- Intentional Leaders know when to speak and when to be quiet. They do not need to say something just to show off their knowledge but neither will they keep quiet just to preserve peace when something important is at stake.

- Intentional Leaders go out of their own comfort zone to grow and develop new knowledge and skills. They do not remain passive and stagnant.

- Intentional Leaders are always hungry to learn rather than assuming that they know it all. They ask how things could be done better the next time rather than settle for the status quo.

- Intentional Leaders lead with questions and not just with answers. They build and empower teams around the organization and not around themselves. They are on the constant lookout for successors.

- Intentional Leaders lead with the end in mind. The legacy they leave behind is in people and not merely in projects.

Leadership makes or breaks an organization. Are you an intentional leader? Don't just go through the motions.

Are you leading by design or by default?

Questions for Reflection

1. Explain what is meant when we say a person did something by design, not by default.

2. Describe what happens when we consistently do things by default.

3. Identify three steps you can take that will develop you into a person who consistently does things by thoughtful design.

Personal
REFLECTIONS

Leading Beyond the Obvious:
Effectiveness, Efficiency and Efficacy

Efficacious leaders are a rare breed.

In management literature, **efficiency** is the ability to do things right while **effectiveness** is the wisdom to do the right things. **Efficiency** is thus doing things the *right way*. **Effectiveness** is doing the *right thing* that ought to be done.

While these two traits are important, there is yet a third trait that church leaders must pay attention to. It is efficacy. Efficacy is not just getting something done skilfully or getting the right thing done skilfully; it is doing so with a view of **God's divine will and timing.**

To me, leadership **efficacy** is "doing the *right thing* at the *right time* in the *right way* with the *right motive* to ultimately produce the *right result*".

The theology of efficacy is premised on a fundamental assumption. We often see the Great Commission as an **assignment from God** when it is first and foremost an **alignment with God**. Jesus said, "Follow Me and I will make you fishers of men."

That's alignment! Thus, the Great Commission is not primarily about a **task to be accomplished for God** but a **life to be aligned with God**!

And our God is an efficacious God.

This principle may not seem obvious at first glance. But if you consider the works of God in the following examples, you might realize the wisdom of efficacy.

- Consider the incarnation of Jesus. Why would the Master of the universe come as a helpless babe? Why not come to earth as a superhero, accompanied by a mighty host of angels? Wouldn't that have been more efficient and effective in winning Israel's heart to God? It was not too spectacular an incarnation but it was totally efficacious in God's redemptive plan!

- Consider the Cross. Why let Jesus die such a humiliating death? While He was painfully crucified on the cross, the people said to Him sarcastically, "Come down from the cross and save yourself, then we will believe in you." Wouldn't it have been fabulous if Jesus had done just that? Wouldn't there have been a revival in Palestine? But Jesus died. It might not have been the most efficient or effective thing to happen. But it was totally efficacious in God's sovereign plan!

There are many more examples: the choosing of the uneducated twelve (why not choose the wealthy and powerful?); the healing of the blind man with mud and saliva (why not just speak it?);

and God sending Paul to the Gentiles instead of the Jews (big mistake, so Paul himself initially thought!). These did not seem efficient or effective, but they were totally efficacious. God does the *right thing* at the *right time* in the *right way* for the *right reason* in order to get the *right result.*

To illustrate, let's borrow from an old adage. Give a man a fish, and you feed him for a day (this is effective and efficient). Teach him to fish, and you feed him for a lifetime (this is efficacious).

But consider the old adage again. This time, suppose that the man is malnourished and painfully hungry. Is teaching him to fish efficacious? We need God's wisdom to illuminate our perspective!

Mentoring leaders must keep this principle of efficacy close to their hearts. Sure, we must be efficient. Sure, we must be effective. But we must also, like Jesus, be wonderfully efficacious!

Questions for Reflection

1. Read Matthew 17:24-27. Why did Jesus use such an odd and inconvenient method for Peter to gather the coin? What do you think Peter learned from this experience?

2. Think of one situation in your life that perplexes you. Why does God, who is sovereign and efficacious, allow this in your life?

3. Name one thing in your life or ministry that you can change to become more efficacious.

Personal
REFLECTIONS

Leading with a Wide-Angle Lens:
Personal Canvas, Larger Canvas and Fuller Canvas

The first defining mark of a transformational leader is the ability to see the larger picture. For the growing leader, the lens of leadership must be customized to see the fuller picture. This is essential so that we do not become arrogant or parochial in our views.

What is sorely needed in leadership today is wisdom.

I define wisdom as "balancing the tensions of life in the fear of the Lord". Proper balance comes from proper perspective. It involves moving from one's cherished personal canvas of micro-perceptions towards a larger, macro-perspective and eventually towards a fuller mega-perspective from God's point of view.

There are three leadership canvases that can help us see better:

Affirming the Personal Canvas:

Leaders worth their salt would have their own views. They stand their own ground. They make judgment calls on leadership decisions. This personal view of things is largely influenced by personality, gifts and background.

Without this **personal** canvas of perception, leaders lack an independent mind and critical thinking. It would hamper their individual contribution to the team. They would be merely *yes-men* in the organization.

Appreciating the Larger Canvas:

But the personal canvas is not without its limitations. For after all, it is but the summation of one person's wisdom and knowledge, with all his weaknesses and inadequacies thrown in. For this reason, he must be willing to appreciate the larger canvas.

Such a person must necessarily work with a team of leaders, in particular a mentor or senior leader, so as to benefit from a **larger** canvas of deeper and wider insight in the company of leaders. There may be times when a person, by reason of limited knowledge, is unable to see the wisdom of the mentor's leading. But a dose of humility mixed with the diligent search for understanding will, over the course of time, yield a more rounded perspective.

Abiding by the Fuller Canvas:

Fallen humanity is but imperfect. Leaders must realize that there is yet a fuller canvas. In spite of the wisdom of shared leadership, even having a larger leadership canvas to gain a clearer perspective is ultimately inadequate. The only way to grow in the understanding of the issues and challenges facing us is to seek the **fuller** canvas of God's wisdom and leadership.

Leaders must thus be more sensitive to the guidance of the Holy Spirit and to higher overarching principles. This is the ultimate responsibility of spiritual leaders. They are not locked into their own prejudices (personal canvas) or other leaders' opinions (larger canvas) but rather, their compass is set on knowing the full canvas of God's purpose, will and timing.

If leaders would pursue this fuller canvas, they would grow in deeper wisdom and great efficacy.

May the Lord help us to SEE!

Questions for Reflection

1. What do you understand about the personal, larger and fuller canvases in relation to your family and church?

2. Why is it necessary and important to move beyond the personal canvas?

3. How can you apply this aspect of the larger and fuller canvases to your personal life, and to your dealings with family, colleagues and friends?

Personal
REFLECTIONS

Leading Theocentrically:
Spiritual, Personal and Organizational

In leadership, good intentions alone are not enough.

Our leadership compass must be re-calibrated. Well-intentioned leaders often fail to lead theocentrically. We must make a paradigm shift from the circumstantial towards the spiritual. A biblical theocentricity (a God-centredness, guided by the Word and Spirit) must direct our leadership.

Spiritual leadership is challenging and difficult. It has become far more challenging than in yesteryear. We become tired and weary. We quickly lose perspective of the first things that are of first importance. Many fail to lead theocentrically.

We end up majoring on the minor.

The principle of **Spiritual, Personal and Organisational** is a priority framework for leadership decision-making. It helps us to put first things first. In facing inevitable problems, the temptation is to rush to get *something* organized to solve them.

We are obsessive-compulsive organizers! The danger with this is that we miss out on personal and spiritual leadership. Often God is subtly edged out of the picture. The "Spiritual, Personal and

Organizational" framework offers three progressive guideposts to help us make God-centered decisions:

1. Leading from the Spiritual

While our main concern might be to make the right decisions, it is far more important to know the Lord's heartbeat in the matter. We would do well to direct our attention to seek the face of God. Let God speak. Let His Word direct us!

Also, we learn to ask the three crucial mentoring questions: "What is happening in my life? What is the Lord saying about what's happening? And what am I going to DO about it?" They help us seek to know the heart and will of God. Then our decision is not distractingly rushed or frustratingly hurried.

2. Leading from the Personal

Our base instincts, our knee-jerk reactions under pressure, reveal what we are really made of. How we think, feel and act springs from the inside. Problems are but leadership challenges that help us grow!

We can learn to leverage the difficulties for our inner growth and development.

Thus, the key questions to ask are, "What am I learning? What does God want to teach me? What am I learning about myself in this episode? How can I grow as a result of it?" Self leadership is paramount. Ultimately, we minister out of the depth of our character and being.

3. Leading from the Organisational

After we have determined the spiritual God-agenda and the personal Growth-agenda, we are ready to tackle the organizational (or as the case might be, the domestic agenda).

We lead by principles.

Nonetheless, there are also standard operational principles, procedures and best practices that we would be wise to give heed to. We put the best person on the job, aim for excellence in our work and look out for the results.

Leading from "top down" (God's agenda), from within (personal growth agenda) and from organisational best practices (management agenda) are the critical "first things first" that a spiritual leader is called to.

Put God first. Let's lead theocentrically!

Questions for Reflection

1. Why do you see the need to change your paradigm of decision making?

2. How do you think this framework can take effect in your life and ministry?

3. What is one thing you would do to apply this decision-making principle?

Personal
REFLECTIONS

Leading with a Clear Philosophy of Ministry:
Vision, Values, Vehicles

A clear philosophy of ministry is crucial to intentional leadership.

Let's define it. The term "philosophy of ministry" is complex because of its multiple usage. As such, an integrative definition is helpful: "A philosophy of ministry refers to the core ministry **values** and how they determine the chief ministry **vehicles** to realize the ministry **vision**."

There are three things that give meaning to the philosophy of ministry: Values, Vision and Vehicles.

- VALUES give the **foundation** that answers the **"Why"** question.
- VISION gives the **focus** that answers the **"What"** question.
- VEHICLES give the **function** that answers the **"How"** question.

VALUES

Core values are fundamental statements of what is really important to us in ministry. They give us:

- real clarity about who we are and what we stand for
- more passion in our purpose and purpose in our passion

- inspiration and motivation that will help us overcome discouragement
- the ability to stay focused on what matters most

Ultimately, we are not just a **purpose-driven** church but a **value-driven** church. Clarity of purpose is but the first step. Resonance of values is what moves organizations. When people clash over how a ministry should be run, the root issue is usually a difference in their value systems. When common values are set in place, there will be oneness in the spirit regardless of how the ministry is expressed in the outward form. Having clear values is immensely important to good leadership!

VISION

Leaders live in the future. Without a vision larger than ourselves, we drift into complacency. Without vision, we perish. Vision gives the leader a glimpse of what the future can be. Vision thus gives the people a glimpse of what the future can be. It allows us to dream of the BHAG ("Big Hairy Audacious Goal"). It creates a deeper dependence upon God. For without Him, we are doomed to fail.

Nonetheless, according to Burt Naus, there are four features of a good vision: it is **realistic**, as it must be based on reality to be meaningful to the ministry; **credible**, as it must be believable to be relevant; **attractive**, as it must be inspiring and motivating to the people involved; and **future-oriented**, as it must draw people to look at what things can be in the future.

VEHICLES

Vehicles give feet to the vision. Without them, a vision is only a dream. We end up as daydreamers rather than as God-dreamers. Vehicles allow people to see the follow-through and concretizing of the vision.

When people can see how the vision can be realized in a specific way, within a specific time frame and through a specific infrastructure, the excitement and involvement level rises. Once people can see how they can participate in the concrete vehicles, the critical mass gathers and the organization will never be the same again.

What's your philosophy of ministry? Be clear about it!

Questions for Reflection

1. What are the top three core values that shape your life and ministry?

2. What is your vision for your life and ministry?

3. What are the practical steps needed to see the vision coming to pass?

Personal
REFLECTIONS

Leading with Competence:
Five Core Skills of Leadership

Many churches and organizations are over-managed and under-led.

Leadership is absolutely indispensable. Yet the ability to lead with competence, and to grow as the organization grows, involves the development of leadership skills. There are five core skills of leadership:

Skill 1. Visioneering:

The **CONCERN** of leadership is the **Future.**

Leaders must have a defining idea. A strategic vision. It is oriented towards the future. Begin with this end in mind. There are four processes in visioneering: (1) *Capturing* the vision (what God is saying in the light of a prevailing need); (2) *Casting* the vision (how to communicate it); (3) *Concretizing* the vision (key result areas to work out practically); (4) *Commissioning* the vision (creating ownership of the vision!)

Skill 2. Conflict Resolution:

The **CAPACITY** of leadership is the **Team.** Leadership is not a one-man show. Developing a high performance team is a vital task in leadership. Developing a learning community is an essential part of developing a high performance team that will last! A strong leader makes for good leadership. But a strong team-leader makes for great leadership. Such a team-leader would communicate and mentor. You cannot be a remote figure. You've got to be touched, felt, heard and believed.

Skill 3. Problem Solving:

The **CONDUIT** of leadership is **Creativity.**

When leaders micromanage, they take away the sense of control vital to team dynamics and problem solving. The team should come together to creatively contribute. These are five helpful steps in problem solving: (1) Define the problem(s); (2) Distinguish between symptoms and root problems; (3) Discover (explore) all possible solutions; (4) Determine the course of action and (5) Do it (execute) and evaluate.

Skill 4. Change Management:

The **CHALLENGE** of leadership is **Transformation.**

In leadership, the focus on results is important. Meaningful accomplishments, not mere activities, are the mark of effective leadership. Change is vital for this. Yet change can often be mismanaged. In leading towards change, there are five key considerations: (1) Develop a strategic work plan; (2) Determine pivotal events (things that will generate the change); (3) Envisage obstacles ahead; (4) Trouble-shoot problems (solve them!) and

(5) Evaluate effectiveness in managing change.

Skill 5. Personal Leadership:

The **CAPITAL** of leadership is **Trust.**

Credibility is vital to leadership. Without credibility and trust, there is no traction in leadership. There are three fundamental arenas of personal leadership development that build credibility: (1) *Devotional*: How is my walk with God?; (2) *Domestic*: How am I leading my family – marriage, children, siblings?; and (3) *Developmental*: Am I aware of my primary gifting in the leadership paradigm – shepherd, teacher, leader – and how am I growing in them?

The leadership journey has a steep learning curve. It is a journey of life-long learning in leadership! These five leadership skill sets would be a great starting point for the leadership pilgrimage. If you are a leader, grow in these vital leadership skills.

Arise and lead!

Questions for Reflection

1. Which leadership skill set are you best at? Why?

2. What leadership skill do you need to grow in to be both comfortable and competent? Why?

3. What must change in your life for you to be where you desire to be?

Personal
REFLECTIONS

Leading with Traction:
Seven Major Processes of Leadership

Leadership is a process, not an event.

Often, leadership is truncated because the process is ignored. We end up leading without traction. The follow-through is lacking. There are seven major processes in the exercise of visionary leadership:

Process 1: Leadership by Rhetoric

This is the most common process of leadership. Leaders attempt to preach and communicate the vision. Yet leadership by rhetoric alone, no matter how stirring, is quite useless. Just because the leader has spoken, it is assumed (misguidedly!) that the message is heard or applied. As such, leadership by rhetoric alone is the common pitfall in leadership. Many fail to realize that it is meant to be a part of at least seven leadership processes.

Process 2: Leadership by Equipping

The second step for effective leadership is to move from exposition to equipping. People not only need to be told *what* to do, they need to know *why* and *how* it can be done. Nonetheless, as important as equipping is, *of itself* it atrophies to a stage of training for training's sake. We are just going through the motions! Thus, a third leadership process must be in place.

Process 3: Leadership by Example

Example explains everything. Examples are inspiring. Unless people see vision being modeled by their leaders, the vision will NOT be embraced fully. Lead by example; not simply by exhortation.

Leaders often stop here. And wonder why things are still not moving. There is no traction. The common mistake is to repeat the first three processes in greater intensity while neglecting the next four. It is like watering the plant with *more* water (until it is drowning) when it is in fact dying for lack of sunlight!

Process 4: Leadership by Mobilization

This is where the rubber meets the road. Unless we *mobilize* towards action, nothing happens! Mobilization often involves leading people to change. It is refusing to settle for leadership agreement and moving on towards leadership involvement and resonance.

Process 5: Leadership by Infrastructuring

Infrastructuring is one of the most difficult tasks in leadership. To mobilize we must decentralize. Moses was taught it when he was overwhelmed with work. Joshua practiced it when he entered to possess the land. It is the old "divide and conquer" principle. Infrastructuring into small groups (and assigning responsibility to each) gets everyone involved. Now that's traction!

Process 6: Leadership by Encouragement

Leaders need courage. And courage is not essentially found in how good *we* are, but how great *God* is. When we see God as God, we are encouraged. Therefore, the chief role of the leader is to point people to God. To see what a great God He is. And that God is on the move!

Process 7: Leadership by Empowerment

Leaders empower. Leaders recruit, train, release and empower other leaders into co-leading the ministry. In this final leadership process, leadership by empowerment, we have decisively moved a full cycle from casting a vision to concretizing a vision; and from concretizing a vision to commissioning a vision. Now that's traction!

Questions for Reflection

1. What is your leadership style and inclination?

2. Of the 7 processes, what are your strengths or weaknesses?

3. What practical steps can you take to further grow in your leadership strengths and to overcome your weaknesses?

Personal
REFLECTIONS

Leading Through Team Resonance:
Calling, Competence, Character, Chemistry, Capacity

Selection is the key.

The team makes or breaks the ministry. Leaders wisely and intentionally select their team. Team resonance begins with team selection. But what do leaders look for? The following criteria may be used for team selection as well as for staff recruitment. You can use these criteria with prayerful discernment:

1. Calling:

God calls specific people to specific tasks. There is usually a distinct, unmistakable CALLING in the life of a person who wants to answer God's call to ministry. There might be a clear, compelling word from the Bible. Or perhaps a sovereign intervention in circumstances.

In any case, there is the conviction of the call of God to a particular vocation or ministry. This is paramount as it will ensure a long-term commitment.

2. Character:

With calling comes character. Character is everything. A person's wholeness and basic commitment to integrity are paramount in ministry. These reveal the inner moral compass and ensure the honor of God and the Church.

No matter how competent a person may be, the ministry will be at risk if the character is flawed. Never compromise on character!

3. Competence:

A good person with good character does not always produce good work. Sometimes, it may just be a mismatch of gifts and role. Except for the purpose of growth and development, there has to be a match in abilities and role. Otherwise, people are not empowered to operate at their best as a team member.

God has given us natural talents and spiritual gifts to be leveraged for God's work. Without this clear matching, we risk mediocrity and the work of God suffers.

4. Chemistry:

There has to be a sense of team fit and camaraderie. This is the DNA or chemistry that leaders should not overlook. It is often difficult to try to change someone to fit the existing group culture. Ensure a fit at the point of selection.

Chemistry is not uniformity. Look for unity in diversity. A person may be a strong individual and yet make a great team-player. It has to do with the person's attitude. Select those who have a chemistry together in spite of being different.

5. Capacity:

Capacity can be developed over time. This is the inner and emotional strength which allows a person to function effectively even when under pressure. The person who develops the well of capacity usually has a deep reservoir of endurance, knowledge and confidence to finish well.

In a world preoccupied with **capital development** (resources of a leader), we are to also focus on **capacity development** (resilience of the leader).

Selection is the key to team resonance. Don't compromise on it!

Questions for Reflection

1. Can you really find someone who has all of the above? How realistic is it?

2. Share how you selected someone to be your team member and if it turned out as you had expected.

3. What is the most important lesson you've learned in people selection?

Personal
REFLECTIONS

Leading Towards Success:
Re-Defining Success in Ministry

We must neither be intimidated nor intoxicated by size.

Leaders need a radical re-definition of success. It is deceptively easy to confuse **greatness** with **largeness**. All of us are called by God to greatness but not all of us are called by God to largeness. The first thing to be said is that our purpose is not merely to grow in numbers. Otherwise, the ministries of Jeremiah or Jesus would be misguidedly discounted!

In an age of superficiality, the Church must be careful not to get sucked into the numbers game. We must not be swept along by an ego-trip that equates numbers with success. It is a common compromise to sacrifice integrity and truth upon the altar of numbers.

Nonetheless, we must maintain a balance.

Size matters. Success and size are often linked. The Bible that says, "Be faithful", also says "Be fruitful". Both are important to God. He is clearly not pleased with fishing without catching (Luke 5:4-11); an empty banquet table (Luke 14:15-23); a barren fig tree (Luke 13:19) or a ripe harvest that is not reaped (Matt 9:36-38).

Nothing is sadder on the face of the earth than an in-grown church that does not grow, in spite of its growth potential. Heir to infinite resources, destined for glory, entrusted with the glorious Gospel, an in-grown church is an irresponsible sleeping giant. There *is* such a thing as irresponsible non-growth!

I suspect that much of the mega-church bashing that goes on is by size-inhibited and size-intimidated leaders. The **size-inhibited** leader might easily lose heart with the smallness of his ministry. And the **size-intimidated** leader might easily lose courage to take the church towards quantum growth leaps.

To mask their insecurities, they swing to one of two extremes: (1) **copying** the mega-churches or (2) **criticizing** the mega-churches. I think we need to **celebrate** the mega-churches (and what the Lord is doing through them) without being uncritical of the excesses and praying for them that God would mature them even more and bless them!

Others are sincerely opposed to the "numbers game". But these fail to realize that the book of Acts is unabashed about reporting church growth in numbers (Acts 1:15; 2:41; 4:4; 21:20). Donald McGavran notes: "The Church is made up of countable people and there is nothing particularly spiritual in not counting them. Men use the numerical approach in all worthwhile human endeavour...Without it, effective administration and accurate forecasts would be impossible."

Count numbers for effectiveness, not for ego.

Success is a purpose-word. The more clearly you can define your purpose, the more easily you can measure your success. Sure, we need a radical re-definition of success. But more fundamentally, what we really need is a radical re-examination of purpose.

Jesus' earthly ministry "failed" in many things. He did not abolish slavery in His time. He did not leave an institution like a School of Prophets or the Academy of Apostles. But what Jesus set out to do, He succeeded in completing. True success is not measured by what it fails to do but what it succeeds in accomplishing.

What have you set out to do? What's your defining purpose? More significantly, what has God called you to do? Do it. For your success depends on it!

Questions for Reflection

1. How is success linked to purpose?

2. What have you set out to do? What's your defining purpose?

3. What do you think about success in relation to size?

Personal
REFLECTIONS

Discipleship

Discipleship and Transformation:
Transformation Precedes Multiplication

God redeems us – so as to transform us – in order to multiply us!

Our God is a God who multiplies. Most Christians see God as a God of redemption (a God who redeems and restores His people) but fail to see Him as a God of multiplication.

This theology of a multiplying God has enormous implications; not the least of which is that the Church is called of God not just to make converts but to build strong disciples of Christ who would multiply spiritually.

The theology of a multiplying God is seen in several places in the Bible:

- To Adam (Gen 1:28) – First command given: "Be fruitful and **multiply.**"
- To Noah (Gen 9:1,7) – Twice: "Be fruitful and **multiply.**"
- To Abraham (Gen 13:16; 15:5; 17:2,20; 22:17) – "And I will **multiply** you exceedingly."
- To Sarah, Abraham's wife (Gen 16:10) – "...will greatly **multiply**"
- To Isaac, Abraham's son (Gen 26:4,24) – Twice: "I will

multiply your descendants!"

- To Jacob, Abraham's grandson (Gen 28:3; 35:10-11) – "...make you fruitful and *multiply* you..."
- The Basis of Moses' Intercession (Ex 32:13) – "...said to them, 'I will *multiply*...'"
- An essential part of Remnant Theology and Promise (Jer 23:3; cf. Jer 33:3) - "Then I Myself will gather the remnant... and they will be fruitful and *multiply*."

Herein lies a grand principle for disciplemaking ministries: The strategy of God is not spiritual addition but spiritual **multiplication**!

Our God is a God of multiplication.

But get this: Multiplication is not the chief challenge of the Church. **Transformation** is! Transformation must precede multiplication!

There is something that is radically amiss here. We often miss the importance of transformation. In his book *Growing True Disciples*, George Barna leveled a legitimate criticism at the contemporary Church. He wrote:

> We have defined 'discipleship' as head knowledge rather than complete transformation.

Mere bigness is NOT God's agenda. Transformation is His goal. Our God is not just a God of redemption, He is also a God of multiplication. But He is not just a God of multiplication, He is also a God of transformation.

In 1986, Roy Robertson wrote a basic but classic book entitled *The Timothy Principle*. When the book was reprinted locally last year, I was invited to write a foreword. This is an essential part of what I said:

> The aim of disciplemaking is spiritual transformation. Biblical Christianity is fundamentally rooted in the transforming power of God to change lives....

> It is a radical transformation that metamorphosizes all arenas of personal and public life. It results in a mighty move of God that shapes culture, transforms cities, impacts lives and alters the course of human destinies...

> This is the enduring strategy of Jesus the Master Disciplemaker. He selected twelve and poured His life into them (Mark 3:14).

God redeems us – so as to transform us – in order to multiply us! Transformation must precede multiplication.

Questions for Reflection

1. "Transformation must precede multiplication" – What does it mean?

Personal
REFLECTIONS

2. What happens if we have multiplication without transformation?

3. How can we be transformed?

PARADIGM 22
Discipling for Life Change:
Content, Community, Consecration

The Church has misguidedly truncated discipleship training.

The discipleship training emphasis has often been placed on content alone. This over-emphasis on content alone might be symptomatic of the Western education system. Increasingly, however, the West is re-learning the importance of community. People learn better in small groups.

But **content** and **community** alone are not enough in discipleship training. There must also be the element of personal **consecration**. These three emphases are our pedagogical framework for life-changing discipleship training.

Obviously, there is no substitute for good **content**. And there are many good discipleship materials available for discipleship training. Find one that is suitable for your group and be trained to use it well.

However, many of us think that change happens when we

know the content. This is true but inadequate. Information or content doesn't change us. For example, the "scare" pictures on cigarette packs (which warn us of cancer) have little effect on smokers. Information or content alone doesn't necessarily bring about life change.

What else is needed?

We have found that there is a social dimension to change – being in **community** is essential. This is because of two factors: first, it keeps us accountable. When we *make* ourselves accountable to another who will *hold* us accountable, we find we keep to our goals better.

Second, there is an environmental aspect to change. We change best when there is an environment that encourages the changes we seek. A good example is that people who join a health club are more motivated to exercise than the individual exercising alone. There is a social dimension to change and community is the second key component to change.

The last component is the God-component – we call it **consecration**.

God in His divine grace serendipitously touches our lives as we desire to change. That's a *'break-in'*. Then we have the opportunity to respond. If we come to the place of repenting and surrendering our wills to God – that's a *'break-with'*. Then we find ourselves truly changing. That's a *'break-through'*!

Thus in discipleship training we need all three components. First, we must feed people with the truth. We also teach them to feed themselves and inspire them to hunger for the truth. There is no substitute for getting into the Scriptures.

Second, we must engage our people in a community of like-minded people, what we call 'kindred spirits'. This allows for mutual encouragement and accountability.

Discipleship happens best in a community.

Finally – and this we cannot engineer – we need to pray for divine moments for ourselves and our people, when God is present to divinely deal with our souls. It is God who is our initiator and anchor for life change. And He employs sound teachings, true community and deep consecration to impact our discipleship. Holistically.

Content. Community. Consecration. When these three components find their confluence, we find the recipe for true life change!

Questions for Reflection

1. How are we helping our people to get into the truth?

2. Do you have a small group of kindred spirits for accountability and growth?

3. When was the last time God encountered you deeply? How can you set apart sacred moments for God to meet with you in a deeper way?

Personal
REFLECTIONS

Discipleship and Philosophy of Life:
Life as Laboratory, Learning, Leverage, Legacy

Discipleship is a way of life. It is not a program.

Discipleship is a passionate following after Jesus. It is not merely a training course to take in church. Rather, it is a life to be lived. It involves the faithful living out of the implications of the Gospel in our life. It is being transformed by the Holy Spirit to live out the redemptive purpose of the Kingdom of God. In all arenas of our life.

What then is Life?

To some, life is a party while to others, life is a pain. Different ones have different philosophies of life. To Forrest Gump, life is a box of chocolates. To others, life might be a pain. To me, life is four things.

Life is a **laboratory**. There is no academic school for life. It cannot be taught as a course. There are no exams to sit. And no diplomas are handed out at the end. Yet all of life is a laboratory. Here we mix and match, stir and blend, burn and freeze.

Life is bigger than the classroom. Discipleship occurs in real time in the real world. When both good and bad things happen, we apply biblical principles to them and see the real benefits of truth applied. It is a real time experience in the laboratory of life.

Second, life is a **learning** pilgrimage. Edwards Deming once said, "Learning is not compulsory...neither is survival." As we explore life as a laboratory, we glean insights, truths and principles for transformed living. We experiment and learn. We explore and grow. Learning is a lifelong pursuit of knowing God and growing to become authentic disciples of Christ. Learning comes from reflection and application. If we have not learned, we cannot truly pass it on.

We learn from many sources. As we learn from our failures, our faith adventures, our breakthroughs and our inner-life challenges, we become better and fuller disciples for God. As life-long learners, we move up the learning curve of life!

Third, life is a **leverage**. The real life applications of these principles give us the leverage for the deeper and fuller life. We stand taller and stronger because we see more clearly. We become wiser through experiencing God. The more we know and live in God, the truer and clearer our faith becomes.

Our greatest leverage for Jesus is our growth in Him. What we learn in the laboratory of life, we can fully leverage it for the Kingdom.

Finally, life is a **legacy**. These precious deposits can now be passed to the next generation. This is our life's legacy that will instruct and inspire the next generation. Much of this is not taught in the classroom. It must be modelled and cultivated.

Leaving a worthwhile legacy, like growth, does not happen overnight. To leave a godly legacy is to leave a worthwhile legacy. It requires consistent effort. Only then can our next generation build further upon these foundations. And grow even stronger in their journeys of faith in God.

Life. It is a gift from God. And what we make of life is our gift back to God. Live with godly purpose and holy passion. Live well!

Questions for Reflection

1. What is your philosophy of life?

2. Why do we need to anchor our lifelong learning on knowing and doing God's will for our lives?

3. What do you most desire to leave behind as a legacy from your life-walk in Christ?

Personal REFLECTIONS

Discipleship and the World:
The Four-Fold Crisis of Discipleship

A "tunnel vision" hurts any organization.

We cannot lead blindly. Leaders need to grasp an understanding of the times (1 Chr 12:32). In our postmodern era, at least four critical concerns confront contemporary discipleship:

1. The Crisis of Identity in an Age of Narcissism

Ours is a narcissistic culture. It is a culture of self-love. Many are lovers of self. Few are true lovers of God. Fulfillment in life is erroneously thought to be found in wanton consumerism and instant gratification. In our vain attempt to find ourselves through self-love and self-indulgence, we have lost our core identity as a holy people of God.

Here's the grand irony. **Who** we are is significantly bound up with **whose** we are. When we draw closer to God, our identity becomes clearer in Him. The more we drift from God, the more we lose our sense of identity!

2. The Crisis of Truth in an Age of Pragmatism

Unexamined assumptions shape the thinking of this generation. What engages the mind is no longer "what's true" but rather, "what works". Truth is sacrificed upon the altar of pragmatism.

The conscience of the mind has become impaired by shallow rationalism. And the conviction of the heart by spiritual deceptions. Yet truth is the most precious commodity in the unseen world. We must reclaim it by an intentional cultivation of wiser discernment and deeper reflection in the Word!

3. The Crisis of Authority in an Age of Consumerism

Consumerism compromises discipleship. Consumerism has at least three defining features. It enthrones our rights ("*the customer is always right*"), it exerts our choices ("*more varieties and options*") and it enlarges our wants ("*I must have this*!"). Acquisition does not satisfy our appetites, it merely increases them!

The spirit of consumerism has insidiously crept into the Church. Many Christians go to church simply to have their needs (and expectations) met. They have no genuine desire to meet the needs of others. Many do not want to deal with the difficult but growth-enhancing exercise of submitting to authority. These negative attitudes compromise discipleship!

4. The Crisis of Spirituality in an Age of Fatigue

It is good to be busy. After all, an idle mind is the devil's workshop! But being busy and being rushed are two different things. One can be busy and yet rested (and refreshed) in spirit. But such precious restedness eludes the rushed soul. A constant sense of rush is a signal of a life that's too busy.

Intimacy with God is sacrificed on the altar of over-involvement. Many are running on empty. We become spiritually dry. Our rushed lives, coupled with our insecurities, eventually lead to soul fatigue. Soul fatigue is a prevalent problem, even among well-intentioned leaders. It's time to turn the tide!

The Word, not the world, should set the agenda for the Church. Grasping the significant trends influencing our world, we must engage our minds in these arenas and take every thought captive under the Lordship of Christ.

That's discipleship that is counter-cultural!

Questions for Reflection

1. Read Psalm 40:1–12. In what way does truth protect us?

2. Read Joshua 22:4-6. What are the six reminders and their purpose?

3. Jesus taught as one who has authority (Mark 1:22; Matt 21:24; Mark 2:10). How would you define authority? How should it be exercised?

Personal
REFLECTIONS

PARADIGM 25
Discipleship and The Word:
Desire, Discipline, Delight, Devotion

We are fast becoming a biblically illiterate society. This is worrisome!

The knowledge of the Word of God is superficial. Even within the Church! We echo what we hear rather than develop deep convictions from a *personal* study of the Scriptures. To many, the Word has become incidental rather than fundamental.

Too often, Bible study has become a place of shared ignorance. We come to share our superficial opinions. Many fail to have a personal, sustained and delightful investigation of the Word of God.

To Jesus, however, the Word of God is of prime importance.

The primacy of the Word is expressed by Jesus Christ Himself: *"It is written, 'Man shall not live on bread alone, but on every word that proceeds out of the mouth of God'"* (Matt 4:4). A Christ-centered disciple is a Word-centered disciple. For the Scriptures decisively point to Christ (Luke 24:27,44-45; Ps 40:7; John 5:39).

To glean from the Word, we must abide in the Word. This is crucial to vital discipleship. There are four keys to this abiding.

A Sincere Desire

A much-needed paradigm shift is to view the Bible not merely as a book of **messages** but as a book of **meetings**. Many view the Scriptures as simply messages to be understood. But the Bible is not merely a collection of texts to be understood. More significantly, it is a book where the Almighty God is to be encountered! We must desire the Word of God as such.

In the past generation, the challenge was: "No Bible, No Breakfast." Today, the challenge for the present generation should be: "No Bible, No Email!"

A Steady Discipline

Discipline in the Word is a growing mastery. Discipline means "to mould", "to correct", "to make stronger", "to train" for godliness. To discipline is to vigorously exercise the body, the mind and the spirit. The exercise of discipline is intentional. It is purposeful and planned.

Unless godliness is a deliberate effort, the fruits will not be lasting and true. Discipline is something you must work on. It is not a natural gift or tendency. It must be nurtured. We need to cultivate a steady personal discipline in the Word.

A Sweet Delight

The Psalmist declares, "Thy Law is my delight." Delighting in God's Word is a cultivated taste. It does not come naturally when you first start it. Savor the Bible verse by verse, chapter by chapter and book by book. Prioritize the Word of God in your life. Delight in it!

The Word is not merely for our information but for our transformation! Therein lies the core of our delight!

A Sanctified Devotion

Devotion to the Word is all about deepening your love for God. God expresses His love to His people throughout the Bible. Our devotion to the Word is a response to His love. Moving from a mere knowledge of God's Word to a passion to truly know God!

Having devotion without discipline is day-dreaming. Having discipline without devotion is drudgery. When you have devotion with discipline, you experience delight!

In the final analysis, getting into the Word is not about ***mastering the Word***. Rather, it is about ***being mastered by the Word of God.*** We are not just to be a **Bible-*Believing*** Church; we also ought to be a **Bible-*Living*** Church!

Back to the Word!

Questions for Reflection

1. Read Psalm 119:9-16. Which verses tell you about the Psalmist's desire for, discipline in, delight in and devotion to the Word of God?

2. Why is it important for Christians to experience this entire process?

3. At which point in this process are you right now? How can you move on from here?

Personal REFLECTIONS

Discipleship and Small Groups:
Four Important Small-Group Agendas

Active community life in small groups is a biblical pattern.

In the Old Testament, Moses organized the people into small groups to meet the needs of the people (Ex 18:21). In the New Testament, the early church met as small groups in homes (Acts 2:46).

Jesus Himself used small groups as a strategy for disciplemaking (Mark 3:14).

A study of the world's largest churches reveals three common fundamentals: *prayer, cells* and *missions*. Prayer is the root, cells are the trunk and missions is the fruit. And where does the Word come in? It should inform and direct all these three. Yet these are the three weakest areas in many churches!

Of these, infrastructuring the disciplemaking church through small groups is the greatest leadership challenge. The disciplemaking pastor must understand the cell group as a basic disciplemaking unit.

The Discipleship Cell Agenda

- **The 4 W's** of our small group agenda are Worship, Word, Works and Walk.*

- **Worship** deals with our _**identity**_. Our identity is not merely based on *who* we are but more significantly, on *whose* we are.

- **Word** deals with biblical _**insights**_. Insights for practical living.

- **Works** deals with our _**influence**_. Influence that makes a difference through what we strategically engage in.

- **Walk** deals with our _**integrity**_. Integrity that lives out our faith victoriously.

This is best represented in the diagram below.

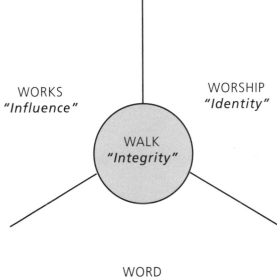

WORKS
"Influence"

WORSHIP
"Identity"

WALK
"Integrity"

WORD
"Insights"

Is it not all too familiar that a sense of **dryness**, **deadness**, **emptiness** or even **meaninglessness** creeps into our cell meetings when we fail to focus on the worship of God, our intake of His Word, our walk in Him and works for Him?

The key to **life** and **spiritual vibrancy** is to have our walk *anchored* in the Word and our works *flowing out* of worship. In fact, when we *begin* with worship and the Word, our walk and works will naturally follow. They become expressions of our worship as we willingly and joyfully respond to God in gratitude.

Hence, Worship, Word, Works and Walk are not separate tasks in a small-group agenda. Rather they are fundamentals of a disciple's life, intricately woven as a tapestry of our love for the One who first loved us!

Questions for Reflection

1. Of the 4 W's, which are weakest and strongest in this season of your life?

2. In what ways do our worship, word and works impact our walk?

3. What S.M.A.R.T. goals (specific, measurable, achievable, relevant and time-bound) would you set for yourself today to ensure your walk and works would be the outflow of your worship and the word of God?

* While the concept of cell group ministry was taught by Dr Ralph Neighbor, the idea of the "4 W's" (Welcome, Worship, Word, Works) was originally coined by Faith Community Baptist Church

Personal
REFLECTIONS

(FCBC) and taught by them all over the world. We have adapted this and added "Walk" as a critical agenda.

Discipleship and Witnessing:
The PDA Lifestyle

Witnessing. It is a daunting task.

It brings a shudder to many Christians. Even "seasoned" Christians. Many of us hate witnessing. Of course, we don't say it. But we feel it. We are not good talkers. We don't want to offend. We don't know what to say. It is thus something we conveniently avoid. Something we only pay lip-service to. So what are we to do?

Let's consider the big picture.

What is the essential purpose of the Church? On the surface, the **purpose** and the **mission** of the Church might appear to be the same thing. But theologically, the **purpose** (the **why** question) and the **mission** (the **what** question) of the Church are two entirely different things. We should be careful to distinguish between them.

Undoubtedly, the ultimate **purpose** of the Church is to glorify God. If the purpose of the Church (the **why** question) is the glory of God (primarily accomplished through our **worship**), then the **mission** of the Church (the **what** question) is to promote the true worship of the true God among the nations

(through our *witness*).
What constitutes a true witness?

Of course, it involves witnessing. But it involves more than just conventional "witnessing". A true witness demonstrates the transforming power of God in all arenas of life. Witnessing is testifying to the reality and power of God in our life!

True witnesses live out what I call the **PDA Lifestyle.**

They live in **Personal Revival** (P), walk sensitive to **Divine Appointments** (D) and respond to God's leading in **Active Obedience** (A). They embrace God's priority for their lives. They witness both by lips and life!

Personal Revival

Personal revival is the key to witnessing. Your love for the lost becomes compelling. You give witness to the reality of God at work in your life. You begin to testify of a deep work of grace within you. And to testify of His amazing love for the lost.

In personal revival, you will be empowered by the Holy Spirit. That's the key! The empowering of the Spirit leads to personal revival. And personal revival leads us to become more and more like Christ. It is unto HIM that we bear witness!

Divine Appointment

God truly gives divine appointments. A life walking in personal revival will be a life led by God. We do not need to run around like chickens with their heads cut off. God will direct us to whom He desires us to speak!

When you begin to hear or see God working in your life, you move where God directs. You become spiritually sensitive and alert. In personal revival, you walk in the divine appointments that God brings into your life. You begin to ride upon His divine moves and seize the divine appointments for both evangelism and edification.

Active Obedience

When God prompts, we must obey. When you readily respond to God's divine moves, you begin to experience His Kingdom purposes for your life. This will cultivate a new spiritual vitality in your life. You will walk in supernatural naturalness and experience His power.

Obedience begets personal revival which begets divine appointments and begets more obedience. PDA is contagious *faith in action*. We no longer have a privatized faith. It's walking with Jesus daily in authentic discipleship!

Go PDA for Jesus!

Questions for Reflection

1. What has God taught you about PDA?

2. Why would you want to make PDA your lifestyle?

3. How would you allow God to lead you in PDA?

Personal
REFLECTIONS

Discipleship and Christological Anchors:
Christ the Prototokos, the Pleroma, the Musterion

Discipleship today must be re-grounded in CHRIST-centeredness!

A. W. Tozer is one of my favourite authors. With prophetic unction, he laments the lack of Christ-centeredness in the contemporary Church:

> The present position of Christ in the gospel churches may be likened to that of a king in a limited monarchy. He is lauded, supported. But His real authority is small. Nominally that king is head over all, but in every crisis someone else makes the decisions...

Then he draws the parallel to Christ and the Church. Reflect on this:

> Among the gospel churches, Christ is now in fact little more than a beloved symbol. "All Hail the Power of Jesus' Name" is the church's national anthem and the cross is her official flag. But in the week-by-week services of the church and the day-by-day conduct of the members, someone else, not Christ, makes the decisions.

I believe Jesus Christ has been robbed of His authority in the homes today. To have authority means to have the right to rule, to take the rightful responsibility, power and ownership of ruling, and to give it to another person who has authority to rule you 100 percent. We haven't rejected Christ; we've just cordially reduced Him and robbed Him of the ownership He deserves within our individual lives.

By contrast, Paul's profound Christology anchors his passionate discipleship.

One of the chief Christological books in the Bible is Colossians. In it, the Apostle Paul exalts Jesus to the highest authority in the loftiest of terms. This profound Christocentricity is brilliantly captured in *three theological terms*:

- **prototokos** of God (Col 1:15; the firstborn, or better, 'chief-born');
- **pleroma** of God (Col 1:19; the fullness or completeness);
- **musterion** of God (Col 2:2; the hidden mystery now revealed).

In essence, Jesus Christ is revealed of God as the *best-est* and the *most-est*!!! (Pardon the grammatical awkwardness but it captures the notion quite accurately.) Christ is revealed as the absolute all in all.

To emphasize this, Paul makes a most staggering statement. He intentionally uses *three different prepositions* in relation to Christ that are philosophically provocative (Col 1:15-18). He said that everything exists **in** Him (Gk. *en auto*), **through** Him (Gk. *dia auto)*, and **for** Him (Gk. *eis auton*).

For centuries, Greek philosophers had taught that everything needed a primary cause, an instrumental cause, and a final cause. Paul declares that when it comes to Creation, Jesus Christ is all three!

The primary cause is the source of creation (**in** Him), the instrumental cause the power to bring about creation (**through** Him), and the final cause the purpose for which creation exists (**for** Him). Indeed, It's all about JESUS! Everything exists **in** Him, **through** Him, and **for** Him.

Christ is ALL in ALL. If Christ is not Lord of all, He is not Lord at all.

This is at the heart of true discipleship!

Questions for Reflection

1. What are the Christological anchors of your life and discipleship (i.e. how do you view Christ?)

Personal
REFLECTIONS

2. Why are Christological anchors important in discipleship today?

3. How can we deepen our Christological anchors as we grow in Him?

Discipleship and Absolute Surrender:

Commitment vs. Surrender

A Christian leader from Romania was once asked a thought-provoking question: *"Why is it that the Church in the Western world has lost its power with God and man?"*

The answer this Romanian Christian leader gave was profoundly insightful. He said, "The Church in the Western world has lost its power with God and man because it has substituted *commitment* for *surrender."*

This is a challenging thought. It goes right to the root of the problem. There is a great difference between a surrendered life and a committed life. It is as great a difference as that between bleeding and blood transfusion!

Commitment or **Surrender**? What's the difference?

The committed life emphasizes what we must do for Christ; the surrendered life embraces what Christ has done for us. Christianity is not essentially DO but DONE. It is not TRY but TRUST.

The committed life relies on one's ability to perform; the surrendered life realizes that we can *do nothing* apart from God. To state it in conventional terms, the committed life centers on our **Doing** while the surrendered life centres on our **Being**.

In other words, the committed life exalts our competence; the surrendered life examines our character. The committed life emphasizes the outward; the surrendered life emphasises the inward.

More significantly, the committed life centres on operations; the surrendered life centers on obedience. Thus, the committed life issues out of good intentions while the surrendered life issues out of God's intention.

A man may be outwardly committed to the work of Christ but may not have been inwardly consecrated and surrendered to the will of Christ!

Are you walking in commitment or surrender?

J. Hampton Keathley III, Th.M. was a 1966 graduate of Dallas Theological Seminary and a pastor of 28 years. In August 2002, he died of lung cancer. One of the legacies Keathley left behind is a notable commentary on Colossians. In it, he affirmed the work of grace:

> We are a society that worships at the feet of a god called activism. Activism comes from a misplaced sense

of responsibility and trust. Ours is a world that has lost its sense of responsibility and trust in the Lord, placing it instead in what we do, in what we have accomplished, and in how busy we are.

These values have become the measure of success, and it indicates a wrong focus, one on doing rather than on being. Ultimately, we must learn that it is **not we who work for God; it is God who works in us**... (emphasis mine).

Not we who work for God but more importantly, God who works in us. We must be weaned from our well-intentioned but ill-informed activism. It is not mere commitment that God is looking for. What then does He seek? God is looking for absolute surrender!

Absolute surrender. There is no substitute for it!

Questions for Reflection

1. What's the most important distinction between commitment and surrender to you? Why?

2. Why is absolute surrender essential to discipleship?

3. How can we be tutored to walk in absolute surrender?

Personal
REFLECTIONS

Discipleship and Sacred Trust:
Into Thy Hands

They were caught by surprise.

Jesus cried out. Aloud. The Scriptures captured that dramatic moment with these striking words: "Jesus cried out to His Father **with a loud voice**" (emphasis mine). Some of the eyewitnesses must have been momentarily stunned. It was totally unexpected.

Jesus the young rabbi was hardly known to shout.

He taught with grace. He ministered with love. He spoke with gentleness. The times he spoke out strongly were when He rebuked what needed rebuking. Hypocrisy especially. But this time, He was not raising His voice to hypocrites. He was addressing His heavenly Father. Aloud.

Into Thy hands I commit My spirit.

Sacred trust. It is a rare and holy thing. With His last breath, Jesus was declaring aloud a sacred trust. Most sadly, the compulsive neurosis of our age militates against such a blessed posture of the surrendered soul. We are compelled to be in control. Of everything. Every time.

Our anxious soul is compulsively driven.

Such a compulsive drive makes it harder for us to really commit ourselves to God. To be rested in Him is deemed a spiritual luxury that many impoverished souls have abandoned. We have sold our birthrights. No surrender. No peace. No rest of spirit.

Into Thy hands I commit My spirit.

C. H. Spurgeon said, "Our spirit is the noblest part of our being; our body is only the husk, our spirit is the living kernel, so let us put it into God's keeping." Indeed, God is faithful. We can likewise trust Him with our education, health, marriage, career advancement, financial security, and so many other legitimate needs in life.

But friends, our greatest need is to know God.

And such a sacred trust ushers the way to know Him. It is thus wise that we commit our very lives to our heavenly Father. Jesus in His final word on the cross has shown us the way. Aloud. In case we miss it. Jesus showed us who we can ultimately trust.

Into Thy hands I commit My spirit.

If Jesus could offer up His spirit in a sacred trust to God Almighty, why can't we trust God with our education, or our health, or our marriage, or our career advancements, or our financial security? And whatever our anxious thoughts are – trust in Him. Whatever our troubled soul holds back – release to Him. That's the path of true discipleship. It's a pilgrimage of trust.

God is faithfully faithful. Always.

Indeed, **into His hands** we commit our spirit. That's the key to true discipleship. A sacred trust in the One who is *completely* trustworthy. For absolute surrender begins with, is sustained by and is completed with sacred trust. We cannot surrender if we don't trust. And we are not fully trusting if we don't surrender.

That's what true discipleship is all about. A sacred trust!

Questions for Reflection

1. Why is such sacred trust so important in discipleship today?

2. Why is God the One we can ultimately trust?

3. What is the area in your life that God is calling you to offer to Him in sacred trust? What would this entail?

Personal
REFLECTIONS

Afterword

Ideologies have a profound impact upon discipleship.

One of the distinct weaknesses of the modern Church is zeal without knowledge. The intellectual integrity of the contemporary Church gradually atrophies to a sorry state of a sensationalized but superficial faith. It subtly degenerates into a presumptuous faith without deep theological foundations.

At the root of this problem is the crisis of theological rootlessness.

Whether we realize it or not, everyone has a theology. Every rational person has a personal view of God. Our theological worldview defines the way we think and live. Suffice it to say that we are living in challenging times. Our Christian worldview is severely compromised by postmodern assumptions and the cultural moods of postmodernity.

Doing ministry in such a world is demanding.

Of course it requires visionary courage (the heart) and enhanced skills (the hands). But it also requires thoughtful reflection (the mind). We cannot ignore the mind. After all, we are called of the Lord to love Him with all our heart, with all our soul, and with all of **our mind** (Matt 22:37, emphasis mine).

I would have done a disservice to leave anyone with the notion that doing ministry is merely about heart and hands; when the very aim of this book is to promote the keen reflection of the mind.

As such, I would like to leave you with a personal, theological reflection in the appendix entitled **"How Theology Should Be Done: The Reflections of an Asian Pastor"**. I do so with the thought that the succinct offerings of mentoring paradigms in this little book would be inadequate without promoting theological reflection.

To me, theology is simply knowing God.

It is such a wondrous privilege for redeemed humanity. Intimacy with God. Knowing the Eternal Father as joyously and as intimately as He has revealed Himself to us in the Sacred Scriptures. Such privileged theology spiritually leads to passionate doxology.

The worship of the Almighty who alone is worthy!

In the final analysis, it is doubtless (to my mind at least) that such

inspired worship, such a magnificent delight in God, must rightfully be at the very heart of all true Christian ministry and mentoring!

How Theology Should Be Done: Reflections of an Asian Pastor

by Edmund Chan

The Architecture of Theology

Theology is a vast and rigorous discipline. The historicity and complexity of Christian theology as a discipline is succinctly captured by J. I. Packer's statement:

> For eighteen centuries Christian thinkers have pursued a discipline – variously called first principles (so Origen), wisdom (so Augustine), theology (so Thomas Aquinas), Christian philosophy and doctrine (so Calvin), dogmatics (so Reformational and Catholic teachers since the seventeenth century), and systematic theology (so American Protestant teachers since the nineteenth century) – that seeks a full and integrated account of all Christian truth. Books developing this discipline have borne a variety of titles – *enchiridion* (handbook), *ekdosis* (exposition), *sententiae* (opinions), *summa* (full statements), *commentarius* (survey), *loci communes* (topics of shared concerns), *institutio* (basic instruction), *medulla* (marrow, as in bones), *syntagma*

(arrangement), and *synopsis* (overview), among others – and have been put together in many different ways.[1]

To simplify such complexity, Alister McGrath pictures an "architecture of theology", a basic taxonomy that gives a theological synopsis and structure to this demanding discipline. It encompasses a number of related fields, notably that of biblical theology, systematic theology, historical theology, pastoral theology and philosophical theology.[2]

Defining The Theological Task

The chief task of theology, Millard J. Erickson contends, is the exercise which "strives to give a coherent statement based on the doctrines of the Christian faith...based primarily upon the Scriptures, on the culture and worded in the issues of life."[3] Important as this task is, we must bear in mind that it is not a restricted one. Everyone has a theology, whether they know it or not, and whether they can articulate it or not. We all have a particular view of God. In this broad sense, everyone is a theologian with a privileged responsibility of thinking deliberately about God.

Theology is therefore not confined only to the distinguished halls of intellectual institutions, where they spout incomprehensible theological jargon from large dusty books with incredibly small print. There is obviously a significant place for theological institutions in the life of the Church but a wider engagement of

1. Packer, J. I. *Is Systematic Theology a Mirage? An Introductory Discussion*, p. 17.
2. McGrath, Alister E. *Christian Theology: An Introduction*, p. 119-123.
3. Erickson, Millard J. *Christian Theology*, 1986, p.21

theological reflection, outside the hallowed halls of academia, must be encouraged to take place. Along with many of its worthy professors, I stand with a passionate conviction that theology belongs to the people. At the heart of true theology is the essential and intimate knowledge of the Almighty God. "Theology" therefore is the devout contemplation of God, by the people of God, resulting in a growing understanding of God's essential nature and will, through the revealed Word; so that lives are transformed through the practice and teaching of that which is learnt. Such theology, with a high view of God that is informed by the Scriptures, is not dry but dynamic!

In the light of this grand theological task for the people of God, I want to briefly examine how theology should be done. There are at least six fundamental necessities for doing theology well. This paper succinctly examines these six basic building blocks; namely, (1) the necessity of theological vision, (2) the necessity of theological foundation, (3) the necessity of theological contemplation, (4) the necessity of theological pedagogy, (5) the necessity of theological holism and (6) the necessity of theological humility.

The Necessity of Theological Vision

The Church faces a serious theological crisis. The ideological virus of post-modern humanism has been so entrenched in our 'Christian' mindsets that our ability to think deeply about the things of God has been entirely compromised, often without our realizing it. Herein lies the severity of the problem. We are unaware of the compromised extent to which our thinking has been shaped by a secular mindset. We accept as a norm the profound lack of willingness, or ability, to think deeply and consistently about truth. We are lulled into a passive mode of thinking which militates against vital theological reflection. Instead of countering the fallacy of secular philosophy with rich biblical and theological truths, and a deep life congruent with those truths, we live in a generation where a sound theological foundation is ignored; or worse, even snubbed.

Unexamined assumptions thus shape the intellectual contours of a lazy generation, tainting the moral and spiritual landscape of the soul. As such, one of the distinct weaknesses of the modern Church is that of having zeal without knowledge. We end up with a superficial faith without a deep theological foundation. Indeed, as it has been popularly said, thinking without roots will result in flower but no fruit. In the contemporary revolution of ideas, what engages the Christian mind is no longer "what's true" but rather "what works". Truth has often been sacrificed upon the altar of pragmatism. Of course, pragmatism has its value. But when "what works" supersedes "what's true", we engage life with a severe short-sightedness that will sabotage both a deep soul and a lasting spiritual legacy. For at the root of this critical problem is the emergent crisis of theological rootlessness in both our way of thinking and our basic orientation to life.

This theological crisis is not merely an intellectual one. It is essentially a spiritual crisis. For at the heart of this theological crisis is a largely anthropocentric worldview that corrupts our whole orientation of life; even our basic orientation to Christian spirituality and discipleship. We focus on the sacrifices we make, the duties we perform, the commitments we have. And we approach the Scriptures in much the same way. We read it primarily for answers to our questions, for solutions to our problems, for comfort to our needs or even for insights to boost our egos. We place ourselves as the center of gravity in life, upon which all things revolve. Thus, instead of God being our foundational security, we ourselves have become our own pitiful anchor. We nurture an addictive dependence upon our wealth, our intelligence, our resources or resourcefulness, and thus become untutored of soul to the call of surrender and dependence upon God. So instead of God being our magnificent delight, we ourselves have become our own fatal attraction. We live in an age of unmitigated, anthropocentric narcissism.

For example, ask any Christian why Christ came to earth, and the most common answer given is "He came to die on the cross for our sins". Such a statement, while true, is inadequate. A fundamental problem with this answer is that it is too anthropocentric. While it is true that Christ came to earth to die for the sins of man, it is more significant to understand that first and foremost, Christ came to earth to glorify God, not to gratify man! Jesus declared conclusively, "My food is to do the will of Him who sent Me, and to accomplish His work" (John 4:34). The glory of God is of utmost importance to Jesus and thus God's will was paramount for Him.

What the Church needs today is a theological vision. We must once again return to the cultivation of a right and high view of God. It is the ability to intelligently and meaningfully examine the condition of life and its presuppositions of thought in the light of who God is as revealed in the Scriptures. In Lints' definition,

To frame a theological vision is simply to attempt to capture in a careful and deliberate manner this 'way of thinking' about God, the world, and ourselves. A theological vision seeks to capture the entire counsel of God as revealed in the Scriptures and to communicate it in a conceptuality that is native to the theologian's own age.[4]

The Church needs to think aright about God. This necessity is a critical one. A. W. Tozer, on reflecting on the attributes of God, most rightly concluded:

> What comes into our minds when we think about God is the most important thing about us . . . The history of mankind will probably show that no people has ever risen above its religion, and man's spiritual history will positively demonstrate that no religion has ever been greater than its idea of God.[5]

Indeed, we need to think aright about God. Life without God is surely a contradiction of terms. As the book of Ecclesiastes reminds us, life without God is spiritually barren, philosophically sterile, existentially meaningless and thus ultimately futile. Right theology however is positive and life-giving. It affirms humanity's destiny, addressing at its most fundamental level the theological agenda of who we are, and how we ought to live, in the light of who God is. The Church needs such a theocentricity that is largely missing in our contemporary culture.

---

4. Lints, Richard. 1993. *The Fabric of Theology: A Prolegomenon to Evangelical Theology*, p. 8-9.
5. Tozer, A. W. 1965. *The Knowledge of the Holy*, p. 9.

The Necessity of Theological Foundation

The very idea of the thinkability of God is both a grand and profound one. How can one possibly conceive God? How can that which is finitely finite understand the One who is infinitely infinite? The divine God is totally and eternally beyond human comprehension. To comprehend God would be exceedingly more confounding than for a toddler to understand a post-graduate philosophical discussion of Nietzsche's impact upon the critical theories of deconstructionism and post-structuralism. It would be like trying to describe three-dimensional realities to someone else when both have lived all their lives in a two-dimensional world.

Divine revelation is therefore the key to theology. It is centered upon the idea of the self-disclosure of God. Thus, neither reason nor tradition nor experience is an adequate foundation for thinking aright about God; for unless God reveals Himself, our human faculties fail us most miserably. The canonical Scriptures, the agent of divine revelation, are the true and God-appointed foundation for faith and theological reflection.

Yet, although *sola scriptura* was one of the great resounding battle-cries of the Reformation, some theologians today have misguidedly questioned the high place assigned to revelation.[6] It is fundamental to affirm that revelation is "the primary source of theology, and is also a basic category in theological thinking."[7] The importance of biblical authority lies in the evangelical premise that "the doctrine of the Bible controls all other doctrines of the

---

6. Cf. F. Gerald Downing's *Has Christianity a Revelation?*
7. Macquarrie, John. *Principles of Christian Theology*, p.6

Christian faith."[8] It is most important that we get our theology right and that our theology be informed by the Scriptures, the Word of God.

Submission to the Scriptures is foundational to doing theology well. In reflecting on the epistemological issues which underlie biblical hermeneutics, Pratt reviews both subjectivism, expressed in much liberation and feminist hermeneutics ("bringing the text to our level"), and objectivism, expressed in much of most evangelical hermeneutics ("raising our understanding to the level of the Scriptures itself"); and calls for an authority-dialogue model which "keeps the Bible supreme and the reader a servant of the text."[9] Because theology is essentially centered upon God's self-disclosure, it is obvious that the basis for doing theology should be the Scriptures.

Even so, important as Scripture is to doing theology well, it is not given by God to be an end in itself but for the basic purpose of revealing Jesus (John 5:39; cf. Psa 40:7). One of the most remarkable tenets of Christianity is the fact that we can meaningfully think about God, not just because He has revealed His truth to us, but because He has revealed Himself to us in Christ. As far as God is concerned, ultimate truth is not merely Proposition-bound but Person-bound.

This is captured in one of the grandest revelations of all: that God became man! This is so fundamental that we can say that the entire theology of the New Testament is centered upon the theology of the incarnation of God in Christ Jesus. The Gospel of John presents this theological premise in its profoundest grandeur:

---

8. Henry, Carl F. H. 1964. *Frontiers in Modern Theology*, p.138
9. Pratt, Richard J. *He Gave Us Stories*, p. 33.

> And the Word became flesh, and dwelt among us, and we beheld His glory, glory as of the only begotten of the Father, full of grace and truth. (John 1:14)
>
> No man has seen God at any time; the only begotten God, who is in the bosom of the Father, He has explained Him. (John 1:18)

The Scriptures as God's revealed Word point to Jesus, the complete and final revelation of God. This is attested to in the most brilliant fashion in the book of Hebrews. Indisputably, theology done right always ultimately points to Jesus. A strong theological foundation, both in the written Word (the Bible) and the living Word (Jesus, the *logos* of God in John's Prologue) must fundamentally inform and inspire our theologising.

The Necessity of Theological Contemplation

Our generation of Christians, however, is largely tutored in theological content, if they are tutored at all, rather than in the art of theological contemplation. The aim of theological contemplation is not merely to help us think more deeply about God, or to think more intelligently about God, or to think more clearly about God. Rather, the aim of theological contemplation is to help us think more godly about God. That which informs the mind must also inspire the heart.

We can neither overlook nor dismiss the fact that in our milieu the theological pedagogy continues in much the same old fashion. We are still tutored by the *lectio*, the *quaestio*, and the *disputatio* in dogmatic theology. The doctrine of the historic Christian faith is first set forth, then defended on the basis of

Scripture and the tradition of Christian thought, and then we move into theological speculation and inquiry.[10]

Theological content aims at imparting information about God, telling us what we should believe about Him. Important as theological information might be, it is grossly inadequate to establish a vital spirituality. For at the heart of theology is thinking godly about God. To many, God is regarded as irrelevant except for emergencies only. People approach God as a "quick fix" to their problems. Many in the Church have drifted from sound theological moorings, searching frantically for a quick fix to their problems. The contemporary malaise of irreverence towards God stems from the worldview that God is irrelevant to practical living. Theology thus becomes the cinderella of the Church, unwooed and unsought.

At the heart of such shallowness in theological thinking is the fallacy of the truncated Gospel and the domestication of God in post-modern culture. To many Christians, salvation is a future ticket to heaven with no practical relevance to daily life other than as "fire insurance" against a future apocalypse and a fiery judgment in hell.

We must return to strong theological roots for practical Christian discipleship. We have a God who is immensely relevant to every facet of life. Let us engage life theologically. Indeed, theological contemplation is more than just thinking about God. It involves godly thinking about life and all its realities (its joys and pains) in the light of God. It involves thinking about man (his highest hopes

---

10. Vidales, Raul. *Methodical Issues in Liberation Theology*, p.35

and his deepest shame) in the light of God.

There are at least three fundamental questions to guide us in such contemplation: (1) what is the essential nature of God and His Kingdom? (2) what is the fundamental purpose of God in the light of His essential nature? And (3) what are the unchanging principles by which God deals with man, to be consistent to His essential nature and to fulfil His fundamental purpose?

Theological contemplation probes the emerging realities of life and the unchanging principles by which God deals with man. The sovereignty of God must be once again declared. Our invigorating challenge in contemporary discipleship is to have the right theology of the Almighty God who reigns, and thus thereby cultivate a theocentricity, a God-centred orientation, in our lives.

The Necessity of Theological Pedagogy

Theology must be pedagogical. There is a vital element of teaching the truth, not just of acquiring it. To do so, we must rise above theological ambiguities. Granted that every discipline has its distinctively technical terms, there are ways of communicating the same ideas that would either unfold their meaning or confound it. I have read theological writings that are lucid and compelling (even though technical theological jargon is employed).

However, I have also read some that are utterly confounding, not because the ideas are difficult to understand but precisely because the pedagogy of theology is ignored; and the author is in fact a rather poor communicator, untutored in pedagogical principles, who has confused the incoherent profusion of words for the intellectual profundity of ideas. In the twenty-first century, even homiletics has progressed to help preachers move from archaic expressions to connect with the contemporary audience. Why would not more theologians pay attention to the communication of truth, since it is important and it belongs to the people, rather than just the acquisition of it?

A worthy consideration in contemporary theological pedagogy is the narrative as a fresh conduit of truth. The story, along with the principles gleaned from the plot, becomes the central motif for theological reflection. In discussing narrative as a forum and motif of doing theology, Lints reminds us that the Bible is not "given at one time, nor in the form of a theological dictionary... It is a book full of dramatic interest and comes complete with major and minor plots" (1993:274). Indeed, Scripture weaves a narrative of God's unfailing faithfulness and tutors our faith in Him.

Consider the narrative as an essential part of theological pedagogy. Most of our theological training operates within a western propositional framework. For example, we start with the attributes of God; the communicable attributes and the non-communicable attributes. God is holy. God is good. God is just. And we teach about God strictly in those propositional terms. I see a distinction between the way the Jewish culture teaches about God, as opposed to the western propositional approach. Within the conservative Jewish culture, at least two things deserve our immediate attention.

First, God is not just taught in theological schools; He is taught at home. This is incredibly important. It is the father's role to teach the children at home the very foundational truths about God. Fathers are to be the theological educators in the family! We look at modern society and discover how many Christian fathers have abdicated that responsibility, resulting in a generation that is biblically illiterate and theologically impoverished. It all starts in the home. The church ought to complement the home (and equip the fathers!) but the foundation of theological education rests in the home (Deut 4:9-10; cf. 32:7).

The second thing that calls for immediate attention is that within the home, theology is not taught in the Jewish family by way of propositional truth. The father does not say, "Son, I tell you, God is good. And son, remember, God is great..." No, he tells a story! The father would narrate the accounts of Noah and the ark, Abraham and his exploits of faith, Moses and the mighty deliverance from Egypt etc. Through these great biblical narratives, their concept of God is shaped. And the wise father would speak with such holy awe that it is not merely the narrative plot that grips the imagination of the child, but it is the sense of the father's reverence for God that is communicated to his children as a profound theological legacy. It's more caught than taught. Indeed, theology can be very effectively communicated through storytelling.

Goldberg highlights that there are nonetheless three critical issues that any narrative theology must face: (1) the question of Truth – the relationship between story and experience; (2) the question of Meaning – the hermeneutic involved for understanding stories aright; and (3) the question of Rationality – the charge of moral relativism.[11] Might I add a fourth: the question of Application; for it is in the application of the narrative that the greatest hermeneutical challenge lies. It is in the application that the elements of Truth, Meaning and Rationality are brought to bear upon the circumstance or condition of life.

The Necessity of Theological Holism

Theological holism is integrating truth with life. Adapting the thought from Cole's article on holistic spirituality in the Reformed Theological Review,[12] it may be proposed that there are four basic building blocks to holistic theological integration: (1) Orthodoxy. There is a need for right doctrines of truth; (2) Orthopraxy. There is a need for right practice as a responsibility towards truth; (3) Orthokardia. There is a need for right response of the heart in truth; and (4) Orthokoinonia. There is a need for the right community for truth.

Obviously, theology is more than just orthodoxy, it also involves right practice (orthopraxis). In the Scriptures, right practice is both the desired outcome as well as the imperative for right doctrine (e.g. Romans 1-11 doctrine, 12-16 practice; or Ephesians 1-3 doctrine, 4-6 practice). Moreover, the aim of orthopraxis is more than just applying the truth; rather, it is applying it for a redemptive and transformational purpose. As Lamb puts it, orthopraxis

---

11. Goldberg, Michael. 1982. *Theology and Narrative*. Nashville: Abingdon, p. 192.
12. Cole, Graham A. *At the Heart of a Christian Spirituality*, p. 49-61.

. . . aims at transforming human history, redeeming it through a knowledge born of subject empowering, life-giving love, which heals the biases needlessly victimizing millions of our brothers and sisters. **Vox victimarum vox Dei**. The cries of the victims are the voice of God. To the extent that those cries are not heard above the din of our political, cultural, economic, social, and ecclesial celebrations or bickerings, we have already begun a descent into hell (1982:22f).

In doing theology, the importance of community must not be overlooked. A right community (orthokoinonia) is needed for a dynamic transformational orthopraxis. For truth, and the application of it, is best done in the context of interpersonal relationships. In any theological discussion of truth, for example, due consideration might be given to earlier reflections, such as the Pennabergian, Barthian and Hegelian worldview pertinent to the rhetoric of truth, and Niebhur's postulation of truth and culture. Nonetheless, I would like to contribute to this discussion a most simple observation: Truth is best communicated in the realm of interpersonal relationships.

No doubt, the most important world we live in is the unseen world, and the most precious commodity in the unseen world is truth; and this truth is founded upon the Word of God. Yet it is the most perplexing dilemma for fallen humanity because we were darkened in our understanding (Eph 4:18). What is of profound significance to me is the rhetoric of subversive truth found in both the Old and New Testaments where radical statements (often in language to shock the audience) were articulated to jar the believers (or critics, as the case may be) out of their theological complacencies, in a subversive agenda to expose the illusions of reality held by fallen minds. And in our fallenness, there is thus a need to engage theology not just by way of individual contemplation of truth, but also more importantly in a faith community of collaborative theological learning. In such a community, there is a non-formal aspect to theological education. It comes as no surprise therefore that "some of the most effective learning in systematic theology courses in colleges and seminaries often occurs outside the classroom in informal conversations among students who are attempting to understand Bible doctrines for themselves."[13] A faith community of collaborative theological learners is formed.

The Necessity of Theological Humility

Knowledge puffs up (1 Cor 8:1) but theology that is done well humbles. For at the heart of theological education is not the exchange of an empty mind for a full one but rather the exchange of an empty mind for an open yet discerning mind. And a mind that is discerningly open and openly discerning understands and appreciates the richness and depth of theological contemplation, such that it is genuinely humbled by the finiteness of the human mind to grasp and comprehend an infinite God.

The aim of theology, as Wells alluded to, is not to "master" the subject of God by the formulation of theological knowledge, but rather to come to both the realization and appreciation of its utter inexhaustibility. For God, unlike the periodic table, cannot be quantified and analysed.[14] Such true and inexhaustible

---

13. Grudem, Wayne. 1994. *Systematic Theology*, p. 35.
14. Wells, David. *The Theologian's Craft*, p. 171.

theology humbles us. A discerning perception of theology is the understanding that it is always an unfinished task. As Barr points out, "Cross-cultural theological discussion exposes the limits of every theological view and reminds those engaged in such discussion that theology is never, at least in this life, finished."[15]

Another aspect of the humbling is that we need each other. No man is an island in the construction of informed theological thought and convictions. D.A. Carson, commenting on the

integratedness of theological paradigms, compared the systematic theologian with a juggler, keeping many intellectual balls up in the air:

> Unlike balls whirling through the air by the juggler's skill, the various ingredients that constitute systematic theology are not independent. Drop a ball and the other balls are unaffected; drop, say historical theology and not only does the entire discipline of systematic theology change its shape, but the other ingredients are adversely affected. Without historical theology for instance, exegesis is likely to degenerate into arcane, atomistic debates far too tightly tethered to the twentieth century.[16]

As such, there is a place for humility to learn from the past as we theologize in the present for the future. The one who misguidedly spurns theological tradition, rather than taps from it, misses doing theology well. As Cole puts it, "Theological thinking is also historical thinking. The theologian has behind him or her the

---

15. Barr, William R. *Re-forming Theology in the Global Conversation*, p.8
16. Carson, D. A. *The Role of Exegesis in Systematic Theology*, p. 39

great stream of Christian thought. To ignore the past would be an immense folly."[17] This thought is likewise affirmed by Spykman who declared that "Tradition is the very lifeblood of theology... No healthy theology ever arises *de novo*. By honoring sound tradition, theological continuity with the past is assured."[18] The link with our theological roots and the ability to hear one another is a mark of theological humility.

Conclusion

To become a Christian is not to engage in intellectual suicide. On the contrary, it calls for clear thinking that stems from loving God with all that we are, including a love that is sustained and nourished by right thinking. As Wolfhart Pannenberg has aptly commented: "Argumentation and the operation of the Holy Spirit are not in competition with each other. In trusting in the Holy Spirit Paul in no way spared himself thinking or arguing."[19] There is no place for anti-intellectualism in Christianity. The greatest need of this generation is the intentional development of biblically grounded, theologically sound and spiritually vital disciples of Christ.

As such, theological leadership is vital to the health of the contemporary Church. We must do what we can to strengthen the cord. Our purpose and priorities must be clear. The pulpits of local churches must make a radical shift from exhortation or worse, mere entertainment, to sound exegesis and biblical exposition. The rise of biblical illiteracy must be addressed. Sound

---

17. Cole, Graham A. *Thinking Theologically*, p.52.
18. Spykman, Gordon J., *Reformational Theology: Paradigm for Doing Dogmatics*, p.5.
19. Pannenberg, Wolfhart. 1971. *Basic Questions in Theology,* Vol. II, p. 35.

theological thinking must be returned to the people of God. And such theology should be done contritely, conscientiously and corporately. We are grateful that we have the God-given faculty to think about God meaningfully because the Almighty has chosen to reveal Himself to us and to call us into a living relationship with Him. Thus, we must go beyond a mere attempt to do theology as merely an intellectual exercise; but rather, to integrate it into the whole of life and faith.

Though the six fundamental aspects of doing theology proposed in this paper seem isolated, I think of them as three basic pairs: (1) The necessity of theological vision and foundation; (2) the necessity of theological contemplation and pedagogy and (3) the necessity of theological holism and humility. Surely, theological vision must be based on theological foundation. Furthermore, theological contemplation alone is not enough; we must seek to effectively communicate that which we have contemplated for the edification of the people of God as a theological community. Hence, the need for theological pedagogy.

And finally, theological holism leads to theological humility. We increasingly realize our inadequacy in such a profound intellectual, spiritual and communal exercise. Yet the wonderful privilege and the critical responsibility of doing theology today invite us to such a glorious undertaking. For theology done well is both the act and foundation for the true worship of God, who alone is the adored and inexhaustible subject of all our finest but finite attempts at theologizing.

For true personal and corporate worship is the distinguishing mark of doing theology well. And in the final analysis, this is how theology should essentially be done!

Bibliography

Barr, William R. 1997. "Re-forming Theology in the Global Conversation" In *Constructive Christian Theology in the Worldwide Church*. Eerdmans.

Carson, D. A. 1994. "The Role of Exegesis in Systematic Theology" In *Doing Theology in Today's World*, John D. Woodbridge and Thomas Edward McComiskey. Grand Rapids, MI: Zondervan.

Cole, Graham. 1989. "Thinking Theologically" In *The Reformed Theological Review*. Vol. 48, No. 2

_____ 1993. "At the Heart of a Christian Spirituality" In *The Reformed Theological Review*. Vol. 52, No. 2

Erickson, Millard J. 1986. *Christian Theology*. Grand Rapids, IL: Baker Book House.

Goldberg, Michael. 1982. *Theology and Narrative*. Nashville: Abingdon

Grudem, Wayne. 1994. *Systematic Theology*. Leicester, England: Inter-Varsity Press.

Henry, Carl F. H. 1964. *Frontiers in Modern Theology*. Chicago, IL: Moody Press.

Lamb, Matthew L. 1982. *Solidarity with Victims: Toward a Theology of Social Transformation*. NY: Crossroad.

Lints, Richard. 1993. *The Fabric of Theology: A Prolegomenon to Evangelical Theology*. Grand Rapids, MI: Eerdmans Publishing Company.

Macquarrie, John. 1966. *Principles of Christian Theology*. NY: Charles Scribner's Sons.

McGrath, Alister E. 1994. *Christian Theology: An Introduction*. Oxford, UK: Blackwell Publishers.

Packer, J. I. 1994. "Is Systematic Theology a Mirage? An Introductory Discussion" In *Doing Theology in Today's World*, John D. Woodbridge and Thomas Edward McComiskey. Grand Rapids, MI: Zondervan.

Pannenberg, Wolfhart. 1971. *Basic Questions in Theology*, Vol. II. SCM.

Pratt, Richard J. 1990. *He Gave Us Stories: The Bible Student's Guide To Interpreting Old Testament Narratives.* Phillipsburg: P & R Publishing.

Spykman, Gordon J., 1992. *Reformational Theology: Paradigm for Doing Dogmatics.* Grand Rapids, MI: Eerdmans.

Tozer, A. W. 1965. *The Knowledge of the Holy*. London: James Clarke.

Vidales, Raul. 1979. "Methodological Issues in Liberation Theology" In *Frontiers of Theology in Latin America*. Rosino Gibellini, ed. Maryknoll: Orbis.

Wells, David. 1991. "The Theologian's Craft" In *Doing Theology in Today's World*, John D. Woodbridge and Thomas Edward McComiskey. Grand Rapids, MI: Zondervan.

Personal
REFLECTIONS

The IDMC Alliance
A Global Disciplemaking Movement

Biblical disciplemaking is God's agenda for world evangelization!

In following God's call, the Lord has birthed and developed the vision of the Intentional Disciplemaking Church (IDMC). It's not the kind of church that simply carries out well-intentioned church programs. And it's not the kind of church that settles for the status quo or merely goes through the motions. Rather, it's the kind of church that has **discipling the nations** as its core mission (Matt 28:18-20). Everything in its total ministry essentially revolves around this grand disciplemaking vision!

Such disciplemaking churches intentionally aim at bringing people into right relationship with God and maturing them in Him so that they can spiritually multiply and make a decisive difference in the world they live in. There is no magic formula for this. Rather, it is God Himself who empowers our disciplemaking efforts – as we learn and apply fundamental principles of biblical discipleship.

Therefore, we seek to pursue God passionately, and His Kingdom agenda intentionally, to make **authentic discipleship** and **intentional disciplemaking** a reality!

Under the visionary leadership of Pastor Edmund Chan, the IDMC

Alliance is being launched globally. It brings disciplemaking pastors and leaders together to learn and apply fundamental principles of biblical discipleship, as well as to multiply disciplemaking churches worldwide. We are encouraged by the resounding resonance of several key Christian leaders around the world. Together, we can make a difference!

For further information, please visit our IDMC website at www.idmc.org.sg. You can make a difference too!

Additional Resources by Edmund Chan

Sermon On The Mount
28 audio sermons by Edmund Chan

Go straight to God's Word and unpack the teachings of Jesus. Authentic discipleship from the inside-out! This is our most popular sermon series, not because it tells our carnal nature what we like to hear, but because it is life-transforming!

Ecclesiastes
32 audio sermons by Edmund Chan

How desperately we need wisdom...but wisdom has been adulterated, diluted in our world of information-overload! Returning to God's Word from ancient times, listen to deep wisdom made relevant for today. A great resource for every disciple of Christ!

A Certain Kind
7 audio/video sessions by Edmund Chan

Authentic discipleship and intentional disciplemaking are the biblical keys to raising up spiritually-qualified leaders. Journey with Edmund Chan as he brilliantly unfolds a global vision: "Returning the Church to its disciplemaking roots – through authentic discipleship and intentional disciplemaking – so as to reproduce disciples of 'a certain kind' and to multiply them to win the world for Christ!"

COVENANT RESOURCES

For further information on a wide variety of audio and video messages, please email us at resources@cefc.org.sg